PUT THE KETTLE ON
And Other Cultural Disconnections

Essays
By Tracey O'Shaughnessy

EQUA
PRESS
Cheshire, Connecticut

Front Cover Art: Danielle Mailer
Back Cover Photograph: Erin Covey

Credits: Portions of this book were previously
published in *The Republican-American*, Waterbury, CT

ISBN-13: 978-1523820320

DEDICATION

For Paul James
......who is my Christmas morning

And I shall have some peace there,
for peace comes dropping slow,
Dropping from the veils of the morning
to where the cricket sings;
There midnight's all a glimmer,
and noon a purple glow,
And evening full of the linnet's wings.

—William Butler Yeats

TABLE OF CONTENTS

COLUMNS

ESSAYS, SPEECHES

Put the Kettle On

My grandmother was not a warm and affectionate person.

Her hugs were flaccid. Her kisses were dry. Any sort of physical affection she displayed—and she *did* display it, in spite of herself—was perfunctory and awkward. My mother, raised by Italian-American parents, used to say that the Irish were "cold fish," which was both unkind and untrue. If I learned anything from my grandmother—and I learned most of all that was valuable from her—it was that physical affection was no barometer on the density of love. Affection bubbled up in all sorts of other ways.

Of the many minor cruelties I endured in girlhood, only one prompted me to get up and leave my father's house. I was in my late teens. It was a summer's day. And I, stung by an intemperate remark that landed astringently on an already festering wound, found myself crying great buckets of tears as I walked down the gentle valley from my father's house to the broad, steep boulevard that led to my grandmother's house.

I had never relied before on my grandmother to salve my erratic emotional distress. She was a person who liked a lot of fun—silly jokes and anim   ated pantomimes of absurd stories. So I tried to pull myself together before winding my way up the gray, creaky linoleum steps that led to her den. It was fruitless. By the time I had surprised her and my uncle, with whom she lived, I was a mess. A phlegmy, hammy, adolescent mess. And my grandmother, whom I had always presumed to be maladroit at these sorts of upsets, took one look at me, grabbed hold of my hand and said to my uncle, "Honey, put the kettle on."

The kettle—a $2 utilitarian number she had picked up at the A & P—was the great pacifier of my grandmother's house. When it sat under the licking blue flames of her Westinghouse stove, it meant that a talk was to be had—a serious talk. The kettle's shrill caterwauling signaled complete, engrossed attention by my grandmother. As my uncle dutifully but nervously poured its contents over the Salada tea bag, my grandmother would clutch my hand, fix me with her steel gray-blue eyes and say, "Now, darlin,' tell me every little thing. Start from the beginning."

And I did. And I would. And we would sit there, the two of us, in front of a TV table embellished with a teal blue Venice gondola scene and drink cup after cup of milky, lukewarm tea, into which I would dip hunk after mouth-watering hunk of chocolate chip bars. By afternoon, the Million Dollar Movie was on, my grandmother was telling me a story about John Forsythe and I was miraculously assuaged.

I wish I could remember what in heavens name my grandmother told me. I wish I could remember so that when my son comes home in a similar tizzy some day, I could impart the same lesson to him. But, instead, I just remember the feel of my grandmother's cool, dry palms, the flinty abrasion of her Lee Clip-on Nails and that unflinching, riveting stare that seemed so intent on spiraling right into the maw of my grief to understand it, live within it, and thereby cure it.

For years, I tried to find a kettle just that cheap with a whistle just that shrill, but I never managed it. I found kettles that shrieked and kettles the honked and kettles that emitted a plaintive melody like something out of Handel, but I could never quite mimic that piercing, oddly comforting wail. No matter. It was not, of course, the kettle that I missed.

I thought of that kettle and those long, embracing afternoons when I read the results of a recent Pew Research study about young adults and use of cell phones. Among those 18 to 24 year olds with cell phones—which is to say virtually all of them—some 98 percent use their cell phones during get-togethers with their friends. They are, physically speaking, *with* their friends, but they are not present, not in any real emotional way. While in social settings, 82 percent of young adults read text messages sent by others. Well, there's a lot to plow through. Most of them are getting 67 texts a day—2,022 texts a month. The phone, our umbilical cord to the technological reality show that runs ceaselessly in our orbit, has become a convenient prop for utter disengagement.

"When you're not looking the person in their eyes, you can say a lot more," one 17-year-old senior told The *Republican-American* last week. "There's a space in between you where you don't necessarily have to see their reaction."

Let's read that one more time. You can say more when you're not looking in a person's eyes.

In the past 25 years, we've seen an increase in anxiety and depression among teens. About a third of all teens will experience anxiety during adolescence. All of the usual suspects—saturation from the media, increasing numbers of kids growing up with one parent, escalating pressure to attend expensive colleges—can be drawn and quartered for blame. But the inability to connect on a physical, interpersonal level with someone who can draw you in and hold your hand is an emotional deficit that only exacerbates our isolation.

Sherry Turkle, an M.I.T. professor who has studied the psychology of online connectivity for more than 30 years, writes that college students have developed what they call the "rule of three" when having a group conversation. Members of the group have to check that at least three people are paying attention (and not looking at their devices) before you allow yourself to look down at your phone. "So conversation proceeds," she writes, "but with different people having their heads up at different times. The effect is what you would expect: Conversation is kept relatively light, on topics where people feel they can drop in and out."

John Ruskin speaks of appreciating the "rests" in music as places as integral to music as the notes themselves. I think of those rests as the pauses in conversation in which we meet the eye of our friend and, in silence, decipher their gaze with empathy utterly dependent on human encounter. Turkle points to studies that find that the mere presence of a nearby phone changes what people talk about and the degree of connection they feel. I'm certainly averse to discussing something unsettling or revealing when I'm aware that someone's phone is about to bleat—and, worse, that they'll answer it.

In E.M. Forster's dystopian novella "The Machine Stops Here," a boy living in a community of isolated cells, where individuals are dependent on machines, tries to reach out to his mother. "I hear something like you through this telephone, but I do not hear you. That is why I want you to come. Pay me a visit, so that we can meet face to face, and talk about the hopes that are in my mind," he says.

That's roughly the request one 15-year-old Turkle interviewed expressed to his father, whom he asked to stop clicking on his phone. "Daddy," she said. "Stop Googling.

I want to talk to you."

In a month or so, I am to travel north to Massachusetts for a reliably manic family gathering. My nieces and nephews will parade in from their tournaments and practices, recitals and lessons, all of them armed with one device or another, the protective armor without which they never leave home. They don't like the "boring bits" of get-togethers, they explain. The devices are the connective tissue of their lives, ever at the ready to distract, veil and disarm.

We have about as much chance of eliminating cell phones as I do of having those afternoons with my grandmother back. But every now and then, it would be refreshing if—only for a dinner—we could all collectively disarm ourselves of these intrusive apparatuses and somebody could just say simply, "Honey, put the kettle on."

Publication Date: November 15, 2015

The World Looks So Much Better from Equa

My son has an imaginary world. As fantasy goes, "Equa" is a fairly rigorous place. Chain stores are forbidden, as are SUVs, with a particularly draconian penalty for Hummers. Transportation is via monorail and the entire government is run by penguins, which, at this rate, may be an improvement over ours.

In Equa, there is neither poverty nor wealth nor pollution. The fee for littering is three seeds, planted at your own labor and expense wherever the offense occurred. The Equa legislature consists of a flock of sagacious penguins called senators. There is a senator for exports, and one for art and sculpture. There are senators for food, architecture and one for peace. Seven highly evolved penguins comprise the Equa court.

Oh, yes, and no one dies.

As utopias go, I have no quibble with Equa. It seems a civil, clean, courteous place. The diet may be a tad too fishy for my taste, but in a world of unbridled peace and eternal life, I may be able to stomach a few herrings.

For years, child development experts considered a child's imagination as a benign alternative to a reality over which children had virtually no control. But increasingly, the *Wall Street Journal* reports, experts are examining the role imagination plays in our understanding of reality.

Imagination, these experts say, is not merely the indulgent fancy of childhood, but a critical cornerstone of intelligent adult behavior.

Understanding what goes on today in Helmand Province, for example, takes a heaping dose of imagination, given that most of us will never see the place firsthand. And, as it is with the distant present, so too with the past. "Whenever you think about the Civil War or the Roman Empire or possibly God, you're using your imagination," says Paul Harris, a development psychologist and graduate school professor at Harvard University.

Those of us unable to conjure Hogwarts wizardry out of thin air or splatter Picasso's "Les Demoiselles d'Avignon" on a canvas often react with an awe-soaked envy to others whose imagination seems so facile and rich. But perhaps we are confusing imagination and talent. Or perhaps our definition of imagination is too limited.

Researchers say that fantasy-play in childhood is a stunning predictor of all sorts of positive attributes. They find that preschoolers who have imaginary friends are more creative, have greater social understanding and are better at taking the perspective of others. Imagination, reports Marjorie Taylor, author of *Imaginary Companions and the Children Who Create Them*, is a stress-buster. Children, she tells the newspaper, "can fix (a) problem with their imagination."

Earlier this year, Alison Gopnik published *The Philosophical Baby: What Children's Minds Tell Us About Truth, Love and the Meaning of Life.*

Gopnik's subtitle, and some of her assertions, are a bit overstated, but she, too, affirms that imagination is a critical component in helping us navigate through the brambles of the real world. It is worth noting that the Sept. 11, 2001 attacks exposed many of the country's weaknesses, but its most hazardous, as the authors of the 9/11 terrorist report stressed, was our "failure of imagination."

For a while when he was much younger, my son had an imaginary friend named Joey. Joey was my son's age, but there the resemblances stopped. He lived in a New Jersey city, sold bagels in his family store and was blond, brown-eyed and Jewish. For a while, I wondered about the relative exoticness of Joey but then I realized the critical function my son's brain was performing: By having a friend so unlike himself, P.J. was preparing himself for social encounters he was unlikely to have at 4, but very likely to have at 14 or 40.

Gopnik concurs, noting that children who have imaginary friends tend to be better at predicting the thoughts and feelings of actual people. In this way, empathy — the quality most critical to the flowering of peace — is cultivated in the pliant folds of imagination.

For weeks after the emergence of Equa in my son's imagination, I harbored a sense of guilt that he had created his world as an antidote to this one. The world into which I had brought him was fraught with war, pollution, decay, mortality and coarseness. I had prayed his birth would mitigate these sour realities, but it seemed his only method of parrying them was to negate them and create a substitute world of his own.

I wonder if in the end, though, it is this whimsy that is childhood's great gift. We all need imagination to wriggle out of the carcass of old beliefs and ossified assumptions. My son should preserve his as he confronts the nettles of a world that can seem cynical and bleak. And I, and so many others, would do well to retrieve that spigot of childhood fancy maturity has wrung shut.

Publication date: Sunday, April 04, 2010

Son's Clarinet Produces an Ode to Joy

My son has started music lessons. Each afternoon, he pulls a small, James Bond-type suitcase out of the closet and assembles a shiny black clarinet at my kitchen table.

For the next scrupulously enforced 15 minutes, the house is a cacophony of bleats, brays, toots and screeches that inspires my hound dog to let loose with an aria all his own. It is not every day that you realize your mutt has perfect pitch and has been longing to jam with your 10-year-old.

Over the months that my son has dutifully adhered to this schedule, the dissonant sounds grew more tuneful, the squeaks fewer and the squeals more melodic. I could identify folk tunes, now consigned almost exclusively to elementary school gyms. I heard "Hot Cross Buns," a ditty I remember playing on the recorder in Miss Brandeis' music class. I heard "Frère Jacques" and "Au Claire de la Lune," jingles that once plinked from a plastic Fisher Price radio affixed to the side of my son's crib. I heard — stunningly — a sliver of Beethoven's "Ode to Joy."

"P.J.," I said. "I know that song."

"It's Beethoven," he said, helpfully.

"Yes," I said, leading him to the music cabinet, where we pull out a CD of Leonard Bernstein conducting the Berlin Philharmonic. We slip the CD into the player like a piece of toast. At dinner, Beethoven is our guest, his symphony wafting over us like an autumn breeze. P.J. stares into space, his eyes widening in recognition when the famous chorus sounds. "That's my part!" he said.

And with that, my son became part of the symphony of musicians and would-be musicians who have ever picked up an instrument, sat down at a piano, held a bow in their fingers and insinuated themselves into the great opus of human musical achievement.

It is a group to which I regrettably did not belong. Apart from my brief recorder indulgence in the fourth grade, I stayed away from music, not entirely by choice. My mother, a nightclub singer, was a kind of musician, and during the early 1970s, she taught guitar to a neighborhood girl commonly referred to as "slow." This girl was a whiz on the guitar, however, and I can see her with my mother in our knotty pine kitchen. As my mother barked out "Thumb-brush-a-thumb-brush-a," the girl strummed fluidly away to "Happy Together" by The Turtles.

Though I asked frequently for lessons, my mother rebuffed my requests, explaining that parents were poor teachers of their children, an axiom of her own making. "Is that like doctors not being able to operate on their own children?" I asked. "You got it, kid," she said.

Though I regret my lack of musical training, I do not blame my mother for it. It was my mother who gave me my love of music, of Berlin and Porter, Rodgers and Hart, Gershwin and Arlen. Years later, while interviewing a piano prodigy outside Washington, D.C., I asked whether the girl looked on her proficiency as a gift. No, she said, it was not the ability to play that was a gift; it was the ability to appreciate music that was the real blessing.

Today, I hear about all manner of collateral academic benefits of music education. Kids involved in music score higher on standardized tests, perform better at mathematics, enjoy better verbal skills and may even have more acute memories.

I wonder if my grandmother thought about all of that when she assembled dozens of books of S & H Green Stamps to purchase the organ that sat in her living room. I wonder if she considered it as she plinked out "Alley Cat" while we kicked our way through the Hully Gully. I wonder if my mother realized it, belting out "Call Me Irresponsible" from the laundry room, her voice curling out of the heating vents on the floor.

At church now, my son picks up the bright red hymnal at the end of the pew, thumbs through the pages and places his index finger on the staff. I watch him trace the notes as the chorus sings, his little finger dancing on glyphs that look like Cyrillic to me. "That's a quarter note," he whispers, tapping the music gently. "We learned that."

To myself I say a silent prayer that this hunger for music remains unsated. My son will speak a new language soon, one I cannot speak but to which I can listen, as a grateful audience member, appreciating his gift.

Publication date: July 01, 2012

Teaching Us With Four Paws

For a long time, I had an old dog. My old dog didn't run any more. His leg buckled one day about 5 years ago, and he went lame. He had been fielding a tennis ball, among his favorite amusements, and he looked up at me with a mixture of fear and apology and I knew he would never run again.

We had the leg repaired — but it was never the same. He never did run again with that ferocious fluency he had as a young dog. The way his shoulders muscled forward and the lean sinews of his belly stretched elegantly over the grass. Oh, he was beautiful to watch.

But when his left leg went, his right swiftly followed, so that when I touched his hind quarters his bones felt like dozens of little stones zippered into a purse of fur.

When he looked up at me, after he tore his ligaments irreparably, I remembered the first time I took him to the forest to run. He frolicked so hard and wantonly that he didn't notice the ravine until he was chest deep in it. He yelped, and I ran, finding him sitting plaintively in a pool of mud, his right front paw proffered up to me as if in supplication.

I scrambled down the embankment and held his paw in my hand, feeling his coarse, plump paw pads to assess the damage. He looked at me with his chocolate brown eyes as if inquiring the extent of the damage. I rubbed his paw and nodded. "It's OK, Sam." With that, he leapt up the embankment, clawing at the rooted clay and sprinting ahead to the copse, free and exultant.

Never before or since had a touch from me healed any living thing.

So when he became old and limped and panted and slept so much more than he fetched, I found new, less exhausting ways to love. That is what you do when your loved ones age. You don't ask about hikes or tours or concerts or diversions more exhausting than comforting. You ratchet down. You soften. You rub their bellies and scratch their ears. You see their snouts widen in what you think resembles a smile. You rest your head against their chest and close your eyes as their hearts beat low and steady. You understand the wisdom of silence; it's words that make us stumble.

We all know how these stories end. We know it from the beginning. But we do it anyway.

When I brought Sam home from a shelter 14 years ago, my beloved father, now gone, said to me, "I want you to know that if you get a dog, you're going to have a lot of dogs." Sam was only a puppy but my father was trying to steel me, to protect me, inure me from inevitability. To love, he was trying to say, is to lose.

But in those days, Sam was young and spry and invincible and bounding with curiosity and life. He could hear then, and every wail of a siren was followed by his yawning, plaintive howl, such that I could not think of a fire engine without instinctively waiting for his response.

So, too, with yogurt, which I probably shouldn't have given Sam, but did. Not a lot — just the dregs of the plastic container my spoon could not reach. Sam would take it in his teeth to some dark lair, where he would prop the yogurt cup between his two paws and ravage the insides with his long, elastic tongue.

When he went deaf and could no longer react to words like "squirrel," no rhythm was lost between us because by then we knew each other better than most humans could ever know another. He could no longer lunge upward onto the bed and lay his wet, bearded chin on my chest. But he would sidle up to my legs and with a low, hesitant wag; offer an ear to nuzzle or a belly to rub.

Not long after we adopted him, I realized that Sam was a better Christian than I'd ever be. He was devoid of temper, pride or envy. He forgave promptly and completely. His instinct was love. It was not something he had to work at.

Mostly, Sam taught me how to be old and that being old and brittle is not a cause for pity or regret, but an opportunity for solicitude and a tenderness youth so often neglects.

What did he know about death, I wonder, that I have yet to grasp? He knew that at some point, it is time to accept with grace an inevitability that spares none of us.

I still listen for him, the tap of his claws on the wood floor, the panting of an old dog exhausted by the effort, but needing it too, because to be near us was the closest to happiness he would find.

I am hollow now in the place he filled, yearning for the lessons he still had to teach.

Publication date: Sunday, July 12, 2009

The Erosion of Empathy

A Connecticut television station recently reported that a 12-year-old boy brought a BB gun and slingshot into school to protect himself from bullies. The report came just ahead of a state conference on bullying that concluded that a quarter of Connecticut students had been victims of bullying.

This, in the minds of many, is cause for alarm. Bullying is the current cause célèbre in American schools, right behind our souring scores in science and mathematics. If you're a parent who wants the attentive ear of the school administration, whisper the word "bully" to the principal and watch the panic.

School administrators have every right to be on high alert for bullying behavior. Victims are terrified, depressed, even suicidal. A young Irish immigrant girl, ceaselessly berated by merciless, prepubescent goons, killed herself in Massachusetts, evidently unable to endure the taunts. A gifted Rutgers University violist, whose roommate posted a salacious homosexual video of him on the Internet, plunged to his death from the George Washington Bridge.

According to the National Crime Prevention Council, over 40 percent of all teenagers with Internet access have reported being bullied online. To many who have been the brunt of pranks and survived, such reactions may seem wildly out of proportion to the intimidation itself. But the pervasiveness, anonymity and range of the Internet amplify the assault, making it harder to deflect and almost impossible to ignore. Worse, the malice itself has become a poisonous game, in which the dosage is continually augmented to ensure the biggest yucks.

Bullies seek those great big belly laughs of hate. Where, one wonders, did these youngsters get the idea that ridiculing another human being was the comedic equivalent of a home run?

One answer may be found on some of the most popular programs on television today: "American Idol," "Dancing With The Stars," "America's Got Talent." How much of the entertainment generated by these programs derives from the actions of the talent, and how much by the snide, caustic, spiteful comments of the panel of judges? Anybody watch Ricky Gervais' snarky comments on "The Golden Globes"? If there is a line between sardonic and spiteful, Gervais seems blind to it. Rumor has it that Ellen DeGeneres left *American Idol* precisely because of its venomous atmosphere. Even one of the oldest pro-grams *America's Funniest Videos* mines its comedy from the misfortunes of others. "Look at the guy slam right into the tree! Wow! Can we see it on slo-mo?"

Recently, the *Boston Globe* reported sociologists have found a sizable decline in empathy.

Researchers at the University of Michigan Institute for Social Research reported that college students now are 40 percent less empathetic than they were in 1979, with the steepest drop coming in the last 10 years. Students today are generally less likely to describe themselves as "soft-hearted" or have "tender concerned feelings for others" and more likely to admit that "other people's misfortunes" usually don't bother them, the Globe reported.

That's pretty alarming, particularly given recent

neurological studies that indicate that empathy is "hard-wired" into the brains of normal children.

It seems we are born empathetic, but that the quality erodes over time.

In the wake of the tragic shooting that killed six and left a dozen wounded in Tucson, Ariz., pundits and presidents have been swearing oaths for a less vitriolic, more "civilized" public dialogue.

But as *New York Times* columnist David Brooks points out, "Speeches about civility will be taken to heart most by those people whose good character renders them unnecessary."

Civility, he asserts, is rooted in an acknowledgement of our own "failure, sin, weakness and ignorance."

Once we recognize our own shortcomings, the theory goes, we are more accommodating of those of others.

That is certainly one tired, Puritanical way to approach civility: We're all flawed; therefore, none of us have any business being nasty to others.

Nevertheless, it is equally true that we are all born with an inherent tendency toward solicitude, kindness and empathy.

When society begins to applaud those qualities instead of rewarding their antithesis, we may draw nearer to the civil discourse which we insist we desperately need.

Publication date Sunday, January 23, 2011

The Price of Sacrifice

I attended my niece's First Holy Communion last weekend.

I arose before dawn, disinfected the house, spruced up my husband, scoured my son, plastered foundation on my face, plunged into the car with a pair of balled-up control top hose, and headed north to catch a 10 a.m. Mass in suburban Boston.

This, I thought, is real Christian sacrifice.

As we sped bleary-eyed toward the Massachusetts Turnpike, I tried to remember my own, hastily arranged First Communion, which I received from a doddering-but-dear Irish priest named Monsignor Casey. Unlike my niece Grace, I was 10 when I received my First Communion – two years late. Also unlike Grace, I did not receive it with a host of other seraphic second-graders, led like ducklings to the altar by a matronly CCD instructor, dressed in a sensible navy suit and lace-up Naturalizers.

By the time I received my First Communion, my mother had had several tussles with the church and had accidentally-on-purpose neglected to sign me up for religious education. Call it a divine imperative or a kid's desire to be like the rest of the gang, but I pressed my mother to figure out a way to allow me to receive communion until, eventually, her guilt won out over her ambivalence.

My mother had known Monsignor Casey for many

years and had loved his gentle temper and wry sense of humor. He seemed to inhabit his own religious peninsula, untouched by my mother's contempt for the rest of the church. I believe he escaped her censure because of his bemused approach to authority. Whatever Monsignor Casey did, he seemed to do with a wink, and nobody seemed flustered by him because he was so cordial and droll and seemed to take neither himself nor the church very seriously.

Together, Monsignor Casey and my mother appointed a day on which I was to receive Communion. I was to receive it with my mother at a regular Sunday Mass, without family, friends, or, I suspect, the imprimatur of the pastor, the dogmatic and humorless Monsignor Keilty.

Although I can remember the sense of excitement, the faint whiff of collusion between my mother and Monsignor Casey, my stiff white dress and patent leather saddle shoes, I cannot remember anything like religious instruction that preceded my First Communion. I don't remember memorizing Scripture. I don't remember making confession. I don't remember a worksheet, or an instruction book or the Act of Contrition. I think Monsignor Casey just held out the Eucharist to me and I simply took it.

I look back now on that moment, on the thrill of finally being part of something of which everyone around me partook, and one thought plagues me: Was my First Communion on the up-and-up? Is it possible my mother and the gentle-but-cagey Monsignor had conspired to get me First Communion illicitly? Did it actually *count*?

"I wonder if I'm really Catholic," I blurt out to my husband, somewhere around the I-90 interchange.

My husband does not even raise his eyes. "Believe me," he says. "You're Catholic."

After my unceremonious First Communion, my

mother took me to Dunkin' Donuts for a Boston cream pie doughnut. "Congratulations," she said, raising her Styrofoam cup of coffee. "You're one of us." She raised an eyebrow and glanced out the steamed-up windows, barely suppressing a smirk.

I see my mother in the pew when I walk into my niece's church. It's been more than 30 years and my mother has moved from anger at the church of her birth to a kind of resentful ambivalence. Despite her worst intentions, her three children have become devout Catholics and so she is forever returning to the church of her youth, reciting prayers she is unable to erase.

As I stand next to her, reciting the "Our Father," watching my gorgeous niece on the altar, parents flanking her, I remember the wily Monsignor Casey and want to ask my mother if the two of them were in cahoots that day. My mother proceeds up the center aisle to take Communion herself, although she hasn't been to confession since the Johnson administration. I pray silently for absolution, although at this point, I am unsure for whom.

My mother and I join the dozens of guests at my brother's house, where guests are gorging on prosciutto, spinach quiche and tile squares of cheddar cheese. In the yard, there is a giant moon bounce in the shape of a tiger and an enormous trampoline thumping with children.

I watch my mother spearing her chicken with a plastic fork and finally can hold it in no longer.

"Mom," I say. "Do you remember Monsignor Casey?"

She throws her head back and crosses her legs. "What a *prince* that guy was," she says. "Believe me, he helped me out of more than a few jams. Great guy. What made you think of him?"

And the question hangs there, in the moist spring air, the gentle roar of lawn mowers, barking dogs and the cries of happy, indulged children between us. Just one lesson, I think. Could I remember just one lesson? I finger the cross on the chain around my neck and look in the yard for Grace.

"No reason," I say, shaking my head. "Yeah. Great guy."

Publication Date: May 29, 2011

Only the Lonely

My mother-in-law is 92 now, mentally sharp but physically feeble. She frets over both conditions, chastising herself for her lifelong aversion to exercise and vexed over the fear that her mind is slipping. Our reassurances have done little to quiet her anxiety, in part because if old age gives us anything it is the opportunity to ruminate, a preoccupation that tends to unsettle.

My mother-in-law has lived a long and fulsome life whose trappings lie everywhere about her. She raised four children and buried one, and lives as a widow in the house where she was happiest, like 10 million older Americans, alone.

There is a woman who comes to clean her house and one to make her dinners. There are her daughters and grandchildren, who offer her affection and assure her of her continued vitality but, increasingly, my mother-in-law feels like a prisoner. Increasingly, she wants to get out.

"I'm a social person," she told me recently. "I need people."

More of us than ever are living, like my mother-in-law, alone – about 31 million Americans, the largest number in history. As Eric Klineberg notes in his book *Going Solo,* the majority of Americans are now single and will spend more of our lives unmarried than married. Currently, people who live alone make up 28 percent of all

U.S. households, making them more common than any other domestic unit, including the nuclear family.

It is not as if these "singletons," as Klineberg calls them, have not tasted the fruits of family life. The divorce rate among baby boomers has soared by 50 percent in the last 20 years, the *Wall Street Journal* reports, noting that most of those divorces were initiated by women. Indeed, most of those who live alone are women, who now have the finances to survive on their own if they care to.

Going Solo is Klinenberg's paean to living alone, a manifesto to the soul-enriching benefits of solitude. "Living alone helps us pursue sacred modern values—individual freedom, personal control, and self-realization—whose significance endures from adolescence to our final days. It allows us to do what we want, when we want, on our own terms. It liberates us from the constraints of a domestic partner's needs and demands and permits us to focus on ourselves. Today, in our age of digital media…living alone can offer even greater benefits: the time and space for restorative solitude. This means that living alone helps us discover who we are, as well as what gives us meaning and purpose."

In other words, it can simply rationalize selfishness.

I have no qualms with those who wish to live alone. But to embrace the clarion call of individualism at the expense of community is, I fear, damaging to our civic life and dangerous to our individual health.

As the *New York Times* reports, unmarried baby boomers are five times more likely to live in poverty than their married counterparts. They are also three times as likely to receive food stamps, public assistance or disability payments. As one 51-year-old divorcee told the newspaper, "In the back of my mind, I'm thinking, 'What is going to happen to me? One day very soon that may be me in a walker'."

A study by cited by John Robbins, author of *Healthy at 100*, found that those in loving relationships with spouses or friends were healthier than those without, even when the latter group had healthier living habits. A similar study by a Yale University epidemiologist found that people who were not connected to others were three times as likely to die over the course of nine years as those who had strong social ties.

Naturally, plenty of single people are extroverted and agile enough to engage in all sorts of fulfilling social activities. But we cannot count on our continued health, nor can we substitute the physical and emotional effects of love and community.

I suspect my mother-in-law knows this inherently.

"All this loneliness can't be good for my brain," she told me.

No, it is clearly not. In the coming months, she will likely move into an assisted living facility. We used to believe this was the worst thing that could happen to us. But I'm beginning to believe it is among the best.

Publication Date: April 29, 2011

When Being Consoled is its Own Gift

Earlier this year, a friend of mine contracted MRSA, the virulent infection resistant to antibiotics commonly used to treat such staph infections.

She was in isolation for a week, fed powerful antibiotics intravenously, as she endured grueling surgical draining procedures to repel the infection.

I had not heard from Maria for months. It was not unusual for her to travel abroad extensively, so when my many letters sat unanswered, I was not alarmed.

But when Maria finally called, at the onset of autumn, to tell me what she'd been through, I was startled and a little puzzled. Why had she not called to tell me her life was in danger? Had she let me know, I might have flown to St. Louis, sent packages, or, at the very least, phoned.

"My dear," she said. "I was fighting for my life. Every atom of my being was positioned in that direction. I could not indulge any more than that."

I thought of Maria's silent isolation in late October, when I was rushed to the local hospital with excruciating abdominal pain and underwent emergency surgery. My intestines had suddenly and dangerously twisted as a result of a congenital abnormality and had to be surgically repaired.

In its swiftness and severity, my attack sharpened and leveled my priorities. My son needed to be cared for and certain people — my mother, my boss — needed to be told. But beyond that, as I lay in a hospital bed, fingering the black button that pulsed pain-killing narcotics into my body, who else?

For a moment, I thought of Maria's stoicism, her need to harness her emotional and physical resources into a laser-beam assault on the intruder coursing through her bloodstream. It's customary in this culture to consider that sort of jaw-clenching tenacity as a form of valor, the very steely resolve that made this country great.

I don't think Maria was aiming for that Gary Cooper-style of fortitude, but I certainly considered it. I wanted that same taciturn grit. No one should know. Perhaps I'd wait until I'd fully recovered, I thought, and send out a missive of post-holiday cheer, briefly mentioning this dramatic little interlude I'd survived. It would be peppered with wry anecdotes and witticisms and would assure my close friends that I might have been gutted like a fish but could still not master the Australian crawl.

But the truth was that I was vulnerable and I was scared. I needed my friends — not all of them, but the ones with whom I was most emotionally connected. The realization that I needed them, that I was not, despite my usual stoicism, made of iron, unnerved me.

All of my religious training had insisted on the spiritual merit of vulnerability. "For when I am weak, then I am strong," said St. Paul. He longed for a "thorn in the flesh" to align himself with the suffering of Jesus.

That, of course, is what made him a saint and me a pathetic wretch, suckling a morphine drip.

But then I thought of another dear friend, who called me to her side as she was dying. I thought of spooning mite-size pieces of strawberry into her dry, chapped lips. I thought of sitting beside her, reading, looking up to catch her eyes opening briefly, glancing at me, and smiling.

Only after she had gone did I recognize that Judi had given me a gift that allowed me to comfort her, and that real friendship does not countenance pride of any sort — even the pride of stoicism.

I came to realize that what St. Paul may have meant in his entreaty to weakness, is that vulnerability doesn't just defuse pride, it opens up avenues to grace. When I did write my friends, and relate my episode, they responded as I imagined they would: writing, sending cards, phoning, and even, in one special case, coming over with a home-cooked meal and a bouquet of flowers.

The world can turn not only small, but furious and hostile to the unwell, and the smallest courtesy looms large. Beyond that, of course, I learned — in a way harder than I wished — that, with apologies to St. Francis, sometimes we need to be consoled as well as console.

We often hear that it is easier to give than receive. But there is a gift, too, in allowing oneself to be the object of empathy— even temporarily. One is then far better equipped for the inevitable pleasure of returning the favor.

Publication date: Sunday, December 19, 2010

A Death in the Neighborhood

The Mad River, as it shimmies under South Main Street in Waterbury, Conn., ferries debris under an old concrete bridge ... scuffed here and there with inky black graffiti.

From its banks, a few hollowed-out old factory buildings, their windows huge and vacant, stand sentry over the muck below. The buildings are the kinds of wrung-out, ramshackle hovels that entice addicts, the homeless and those up to no good.

This is a place like many other places in the post-industrial Northeast — weary, dilapidated and derelict. To those passing by, it is a place to avoid, the backdrop to a murder flick, a place not to be caught in after dark. Still, to those who live there — the pot-bellied man and his skinny dog, the cashier at the Mexican deli teaching her daughter to read — this swath in the shadows of the Shrine of Saint Anne is home. The people who live along the banks of this river hang clean, damp clothes on the clapboard back porches that stretch out over the water.

On Thursday, a gaggle of police cars clustered in the broken-down parking lot of the old Waterbury Company, which was once world famous for making buttons. The police wore latex gloves and carried two-way radios and shook their heads. Somebody found a body, stabbed multiple times, in the building, and while neighbors gawked apprehensively behind a chain-link fence, there was a sense of astonishment and horror.

"What happened?" a man in a truck calls out to a skinny Hispanic man leaning against the bridge.

"Dead body," the skinny man says.

The first man raises an eyebrow, takes a bite of a Snickers bar and drives away.

The skinny man turns and peers into the dirty river at a mud-soaked cleaver.

"Murder weapon?" he asks nobody in particular. He shrugs. "Could be."

From the top floor of a brick apartment building that faces the old factory, a man opens a window and a pack of Newports. Two women, the man and two toddlers cluster and gape. An old woman gently brushes the hair of one of the toddlers.

"Que pasa?" a man in a passing car shouts out the window.

"Muerte," says the skinny man.

The man nods and drives away.

From the sidewalk across from the old factory, Jazmine Fernandez, 17; Yamilette Zapata, 16; and Marilyn Dominguez, 17, clutch one another.

"Stabbed?" Fernandez says. "Really?"

The three teenagers had just taken final exams at Kennedy High School and were dismissed early. They live around here, but say nothing like this has ever happened. Well, there was that guy who was found dead in the river a year ago, but nobody has been killed. Nobody has been murdered.

"We see things like this in the news," says Zapata, in a baby-blue Hollister T-shirt, a red key chain cinching her YMCA membership card to her arm. "But in Waterbury? Not like this. The boy in the river and this. Just one other thing and this."

The girls compare all the dead bodies they have seen.

Zapata has never seen any. But Fernandez counts three funerals. The three lean over the bridge and stare at the gleaming cleaver below. Dominguez, a junior, says she wants a career in forensics.

"I love *Law and Order: SVU,*" says Dominguez, her fingernails painted with a tropical appliqués. "I'm, like, addicted to that show."

"*CSI Miami,*" says Fernandez. "I find it very interesting. It's scary, but you have to watch it. It's catchy."

But Zapata can't watch that stuff. Gives her nightmares. "The ones where they kill their wives? Mmmm, I can't watch that stuff."

Fernandez looks into the fetid water and shakes her head. "That can't be the weapon," she says. "Not sharp enough. Only way that's the murder weapon is if they slice you." She demonstrates, dragging a long, manicured finger across her neck.

"I want to see when the body comes out," Fernandez says. Dominguez agrees with her.

"I ain't staying for no dead body," says Zapata. "I want to be able to sleep."

The three girls cross their arms and stand against the bridge. Dominguez is going to write this down in her forensics journal. It will be her first entry. Her first case.

Publication date: Friday, June 12, 2009

SHAME, PHOOEY, WOOF!

My dog has fear aggression. It's a diagnosis, not an oxymoron. "How can the dog be aggressive if he's so fearful?" I ask my friend, the dog trainer.

"The best defense is an offense," says my friend, who is prone to speak in aphorisms.

What my dog needs is to be desensitized, she tells me. Calvin needs to know that friends, relatives and wastebaskets are not writhing, omnivorous beasts, poised to rip out his jugular, but neutral, even loving, ear-scratching machines.

"Let's get Calvin in a dog training class," says my friend.

"Will it help?" I say.

"You don't know until you try," she says.

In dog obedience class, I experience a level of shame I haven't felt since seventh-grade shop, when I inadvertently pushed Cheryl Osborne's bird house through the band saw. It is not so much that Calvin behaves like a feral Tasmanian devil just untethered from the eucalyptus scrub. It is that I, with 25 years of patently useless weight training behind me, cannot control this convulsive, belligerent mutt. I shout. I pull. I bellow, beckon, bribe and beg, but Calvin is resolute in his determination to humiliate me in front of a room full of sweet-tempered shelties, complaisant collies and obliging Labradors.

"Hi. I'm Pete," says a bald-headed, barrel-chested, black-booted fireplug of a man dressed in a motorcycle shirt. "I work with problem dogs."

Great. I think. Powerful Pete has already profiled my dog.

"Give me the lead," Pete says. "Calvin, heel." And Calvin, like the bully in school being walked down the hall by the vice principal, suddenly behaves like the canine version of the Marine honor guard. He cleaves to Pete's thigh. He walks past other dogs, barely registering an upturned ear. Pete talks softly to him, making 'Ssst" and duck noises, as Calvin trots merrily, benignly along. How does he do it?

Just to prove what sort of an Alpha dog he is, Pete does it again, and again, until I think that Calvin has either lost his peripheral vision or prefers exacting Pete with his duck noises than imploring Mommy with her useless pleas for mercy.

"It's attitude," says Pete, handing me the leash, whereupon I go flying horizontally through the gymnasium like a Looney Tunes character exiting the TV screen in streaks.

I learn from our chief instructor Bob that a confident attitude, coupled with thunderous commands, are the key to controlling a dog, which is why Bob howls repeatedly in a roar that sounds like a mix between Jackie Gleason and Donald Trump.

"PEOPLE. PEOPLE," shouts Bob. Bob is middle-aged and paunchy and carries a damp paper towel to capture his profuse sweating. Amid the caterwauling of 20 dogs that would rather be ripping out one another's throats or humping the dog in front of them, Bob soldiers through the room, scrupulously correcting our miserable excuses at walking our dogs at heel.

"PEOPLE. Have we PRACTICED? People.

CORRECT YOUR DOGS." Eventually, he will take some hapless, enervated mutt and zap him with a leash pull. "Baxter, HEEL." Baxter will wag merrily, sniffing deliciously about, his snout open in a big, hungry smile, prancing in every direction but the one the instructor wants. "BAXTER. NO! SHAME! PHOOEY! Pay ATTENTION." Zap! Goes the leash. Zoinks goes Baxter's neck. Snap goes the lead.

"That's a PUPPY. That's a bay-by," says Bob. Baxter gasps for breath. Bob turns to the quivering crowd, a bunch of desperate suburbanites clutching at their leashes as their dogs pant sloppily away. "THAT'S a correction."

Needless to say, Calvin is not the star pupil. Several times he has turned from a frolicking mutt into Cerberus, frothing at the mouth and hungry for blood. I tell myself that no matter how bad it gets, I will not shout "SHAME! PHOOEY" like the Mother Superior at the Magdalene Convent.

What converts me, alas, are the dogs from the advanced class. The advanced class comes in after ours to show us how it can be done. This is like the cast of Cirque de Soleil performing before the Tumbling Toddler class. These dogs can do anything. With the right hand signal these dogs will set your laundry on spin and program your thermostat.

One of the dogs is named (no kidding) Angel. Angel is a 4-pound puff ball who reminds me of Ann Schumann, a girl I went to grammar school with who wore a lace slip under her skirt and was forever chastising us to "play fair." No one liked Ann, but I hear she now owns her own biotech firm. Angel can inspire more hatred from me than any other dog in the class. Angel could make me swear off heaven altogether. Second to Angel on my loathed dogs list is a square-shouldered Rottweiler who looks like he spends his free time doing push ups in his crate. I think he does bicep curls with Angel. I call him Benito.

I crawl hopelessly home and call my trainer. "I can't do this any more," I say.

"There's no such word as can't," she says.

And so out I go, walking around the neighborhood bawling, "HEEL, HEEL, HEEL," like Oral Roberts at a revival meeting. "Calvin, HALT," I say and I see a curtain close from the house of a neighbor who likely worries I am planning a military coup.

The sound of "SHAME" you hear outside your window at night is not a mom chucking her kids' toys in the Dumpster, but one wretched dog owner trying mightily to turn her little devil into an Angel.

But after five months of training, the score is Calvin 5, me 0.

Publication date: December 30, 2012

Stick with the Shift

I never considered myself a tough customer, until I tried to buy a stick. I wanted a stick shift — 5-speed, manual transmission — for my new car.

I quickly found I might as well have asked for a dishwasher on the dashboard.

Less than 8 percent of American drivers now drive a manual transmission, down from a whopping 35 percent in 1980, the year I learned to drive. Whatever gains in fuel economy the stick might have afforded — a measly 10 percent — have been far offset by the ease of the no-hassle automatic transmission. And as we know in this post-industrial economy, ease is one thing you can't get enough of.

I came by my affection for the stick shift honestly. Although my uncle taught me to drive in his baby blue Dodge Dart automatic, the only car regularly available to me was my mother's 1972 pea-green, manual-transmission Pinto. These were the same cars later implicated in several fatal gas tank explosions, which were very nearly as dangerous as driving with my mother on a picture-perfect day under normal conditions.

My mother was a dramatic and volatile driver and my brothers and I grew to understand her moods by the degree of theatricality in shifting from second to third.

A particularly livid mood was easily identified by my

mother's meaty thrust from third into fourth, typically followed by an audible grunt and a racing of the car's engine.

Sometimes I think my mother particularly enjoyed letting the car race there, in the limbo between third and fourth gears, as she mentally assassinated whatever human or administrative irritant was riling her that day. It was as if, during those accelerating moments, she was assessing the choices available to her: an obscenity-laced, full-frontal invective on her lousy turn of fate, or the resigned Buddhist-like acceptance that all life began with suffering and that she still needed a quart of milk.

Perhaps because the car was such an extension of her operatic personality, she was loath to give it up. That and the fact that it was so rarely in the driveway gave me little chance to practice the safe driving techniques I had learned in my uncle's Dodge Dart. "Mom, couldn't I just drive the car with you in the passenger seat to get a little practice?" I implored.

"Do I look like I have that kind of patience?" she said, shifting acerbically into third, the diagonal of her meaty forearm reaching, pinky extended. (The "sarcasm shift.") "But if I don't practice, I'll never learn," I persisted.

She nodded. "There's a Catch-22 for you."

Ultimately, the sheer doggedness of my entreaty, combined with the logistics of running a family, triumphed. My mother let me drive her to work — after a fashion. She drove herself to work and then handed me the keys. "Listen," she said, downshifting solemnly into second, "There's something you need to know."

I drew nearer.

"When you come out of my office park to go home, there's a traffic light in the middle of a hill — a big one," she said. "Some people call it a mountain, but it's really just a bigger-than-average hill."

I began to sweat. I knew this would entail the delicate calibration of gas pedal and clutch — which I had yet to master — and on a hill (or possibly a mountain).

"OK, here's what you do," she said, stepping out of the car and handing me the keys. "The minute you see the hill, slam on the gas and drive like hell. If you're lucky, you'll make the light."

"But—-," I said, the keys slipping through my sweating fingers.

"See you at 5," she said, and sauntered away.

I sat in the bucket seat wondering at the odds. Was it actually possible to beat a light by slamming on the gas? Wasn't it equally possible that you would reach the red light that much faster?

As I roared the gas pedal and sputtered into first, I realized that my mother had dodged any manner of calamities in her life by essentially slamming on the gas and driving like hell.

Perhaps there was something to it.

But, I was my father's anxious-ridden daughter and while I visualized achieving this maneuver I inched inexorably up a hill that was — no, they weren't kidding it was a mountain — easily 6,000 or 7,000 feet above sea level.

When the traffic light appeared, mockingly, in the distance, I did as my mother commanded and slammed on the accelerator, racing feverishly to the summit until, with the slam of fate, the light turned red. I panicked. I perspired.

I wondered why my mother had chucked the St. Christopher's medal from the visor. I fingered nervously under the seat for a rosary. All I unearthed were a desiccated French fry and a bobby pin. I stared into the rear-view mirror at the placid, middle-aged driver behind me.

He looked like the understanding type. When the light

turned green, I ran the accelerator. I eased up lightly, too lightly, on the clutch. The car rolled indecisively back, as if it might rock forward at any moment. But the more I raced the accelerator, the more I picked up backward speed. The car rolled backward at alarming velocity.

I was riveted to the man's expression in my rear-view mirror. He went from complacency to a kind of wide-eyed curiosity, to red-faced anger to horn-honking terror in about seven seconds.

Just as his horn blared, my back bumper nuzzled into his front grill and the light turned yellow. And then, as if the man's anger had some sort of catalytic impact, the Pinto shot forward like a pea out of a slingshot. I lunged across the street as the bleating of the man's car horn grew fainter and more pathetic as the gulf between us swelled.

Good God, I thought. What am I going to tell my mother? But, of course, I'd tell her what I always told her: the Truth. "Mom," I'd say. "I did just what you said. Worked like a charm."

Publication date: Sunday, December 26, 2010

Just My Type

As far as I have been able to sniff out, there are only two typewriters remaining in my newsroom. One is on the fritz and the other is next.

I may be one of the few employees to despair over these unlamented mechanical corpses, if only because I still find them functional, and, of course, am a romantic for their staccato vibe.

I am told there are more of these artifacts on the "third floor," an eerie, unused repository of pica rulers, compositors' tools, hot type, lead letter fittings and, quite possibly, Grace Poole. I'm really not keen on prowling through the third floor, not only because the place gives me the serious creeps, but because I'm convinced my search would be futile.

The typewriter is dead.

Or perhaps.... not yet.

Like most obsolete objects, the typewriter has been seized from the cliff of extinction by a bunch of hipsters who think the retro machine is cool.

The New York Times reported on a subculture of "type-ins," where typewriter devotees gather "in bars and bookstores to flaunt a sort of post-digital style and gravitas, tapping out letters to send via snail mail and competing to see who can bang away the fastest."

One disciple of these "Unplug and reconnect" love-ins

described the soirees as "a jam session for people who like typewriters."

And who could not love a typewriter?

I didn't, at least not at first, when I sat in front of a gun-metal Royal typewriter in the ninth grade, attending to Mrs. Henninger's thrumming ruler tapping out letters while she barked, "A,S,D, F, semi."

I was not a very good typist, or a very fast one. The metal arms of my letters seemed drawn to one another, like a contortionist's limbs, and I spent most of my time wrenching the twisted arms from the guts of the typewriter, my fingertips caking with sooty ink and Mrs. Henninger casting her censorious glare my way. I knew, of course, that success in typing was critical to my career as a journalist and so labored maladroitly away at the task, haplessly painting my compositions with Wite-Out or slipping correction tape into the machine's sights.

I made my first foray into journalism covering the high school girls' field hockey team, and my first belabored report was so caulked with correction fluid that my mother took one look at it, said, "Gimme that," and sat magnificently erect in front of the Smith Corona and began her magic.

My mother was a talented woman. She could sing beautifully in front of thousands of people and she could cook up a swell cauldron of meatballs and stuffed shells in less time than it took most people to pour a bowl of cereal. In a pinch, she could take up a quick hem and knew how to scrub the burned gunk off the percolator to make it sparkle. But I don't think I ever admired my mother as much as when she sat down with my pathetic drivel on high school field hockey and turned it into a percussive symphony.

Her back erect, her elbows at 90 degrees, a half a stick

of Wrigley's Doublemint gum snapping in her teeth, my mother's fingers walloped those keys with a dexterity matched only by the aural majesty of the performance. The keys crackling, my mother's gum snapping, the bell ringing at the end of the margins, and my mother's meaty whack that sent the carriage back again — it was symphonic. With a rip, she tore the page out of the typewriter, handed it to me, and placed the typewriter cover back with a satisfying snap.

I was dumbfounded.

"Honey, when I was growing up, you knew how to type or you were dead," she said. "The girls who typed the most words per minute — no mistakes, you didn't get mistakes — got the best jobs."

"How were you?" I asked, still stupefied.

"Me?" my mother said, plucking the gum out of her mouth and stuffing it into a metallic wrapper. "I was the best."

I would think of my mother in the lonely night hours in my college newsroom, a sinister-looking well of rows and rows of barely operational manual typewriters lorded over by an AP wire machine that pealed out news alerts with the trill of an ice cream truck. There was something delicious about all those typewriters waiting to be manhandled in a syncopated roar to produce something coherent and credible.

Perhaps that is why I still seek out the lone operational typewriter to mash a few words together. I like the thwack of the inked metal on the fibrous paper, the imperfection of the letters, the forceful blurring of the ink, the physical joy of hearing a letter hit its object. Forty years later, my letters are still smeared with correction fluid and sullied by xxxxx's.

But I think I'm getting faster. I think I'm catching up to my mother.

Publication date: Sunday, April 10, 2011

That's Going Right into the Credenza

My brother asked about the credenza. Did I want it, he wondered.

I didn't flinch. Of course I did.

The credenza my brother spoke of now sat adjacent to a fickle washing machine in his cellar. But it had loomed large in the life of my family and in my life in particular.

I remembered it as an august, rarefied jewel of hand-carved mahogany accented with gleaming brass fixtures. It sat in the corner of my grandmother's dining room like a throne. It had one drawer and a mirrored cabinet flanked by two shelves on which my grandmother displayed her Hummels and a Beleek stamp dispenser my uncle had picked up at the duty-free shop in Dublin.

I was not allowed to touch the credenza or open the drawer or cabinets, which only served to deepen the mystery. Better still, I had no idea what real purpose the credenza served — no one but my grandmother either had one or spoke of one.

"What is a credenza, anyway?" I asked my mother one day when I was in my 30s.

"I think it's where the bootleggers stored their booze," she said.

"You are making that up," I said.

"Don't be such an innocent," she sniffed.

I spent part of nearly every weekend of my girlhood at

my grandmother's house, scrambling up her gray linoleum steps, the scent of Jubilee wax and Sanka deepening with the ascent. My uncle had rigged the electrical system so that when you turned the light switch, not only the light, but WJIB radio would turn on. I would run up the stairs to the tunes of the King Singers or Henry Mancini and my grandmother would be at the top step to greet me, saying "And how's my little darling today?" in her broad Boston accent.

She and I would play Michigan Rummy and watch black and white movies from the 1930s and '40s, whose synopsis she had circled in the TV Guide. "There's a swell picture on at 2:30," she would tell me, and put the kettle on to boil.

I was always looking for ways to impress my grandmother, which was senseless, since my presence alone was enough to set her hazel eyes twinkling. So whenever I had received a good report card or written an essay on "The Land and People of Kenya," I'd show it to her, and she would knit her pewter brows and breathe slowly and audibly, as I listened to the hypnotic click of the Seth Thomas and Johnny Mathis singing "The Twelfth of Never."

"Why, that's marvelous, darling,'" she'd say.

And then, in what was real praise: "I'm going to show all my sisters." My grandmother had six sisters who were thick as thieves and clearly spent most of their monthly gin rummy games trying to one-up each other with their grandchildren's accomplishments.

But if I had done something really exceptional, something clearly outstanding that would demolish the hopes of all her sisters' progeny, she would look at me solemnly and say, "That's going right into the credenza."

The credenza was the sacred tabernacle of all my achievements. It was immaculate and sacred. To be placed inside the credenza was to be forever hallowed and enshrined. The credenza held my gilded baby shoes and the first article I had written for a newspaper. It held the hastily scribbled note from my CCD teacher that said I was "a little angel and the star of the class." The credenza held my varsity softball letter, which I had bestowed on my grandmother and a fourth-grade essay I had written about the intrinsic fear of snakes among the Irish — a terror so dreadful God had sent a saint to the country to rid it of the things.

When I would go to my grandmother's for tea and a dose of Bette Davis, I would look at the credenza and imagine it held all my grandmother's love for me. Just as I had learned that Jesus was in the tabernacle on St. Brigit altar, I knew my grandmother's love was within that consecrated credenza adorned with the Belleek stamp dispenser and the little German shepherd boy with the fishing pole and the mangy terrier.

When my grandmother died and my father and brother emptied her house, my brother got the credenza, which he stored in his basement and now offered me in a gesture I considered a deep honor.

Until I got to the basement.

The credenza was upside down and all of its shelves were missing, giving it the look of an old man without his dentures. The back had curled like ribbon candy and the top was scarred by two spherical glass marks. "Mom thinks we can get something for it," my brother said, fingering the lopsided drawer, now fat and distorted in the musty cellar. "I keep telling her it's veneer."

"Grandma never spent that much on herself," he said.

I looked at the credenza and remembered my father, standing in my grandmother's hollowed out den after her death.

"You know, you live in a place and you think everything about it is wonderful," he said. "Then you look around and you realize what it all boils down to is just junk."

I didn't take the credenza. Looking at it then, made me wish I had never seen it. Just as the tragedy of grief is that we remember our loved ones by their last hours, not by their finest, the misfortune of heirlooms is that they are never as precious as those from whom they are bequeathed.

I was right about the credenza. It was a tabernacle of sorts.

What it contained, and the love it represented, was something I had to hold within me, its physical presence so much less important than the place it once held for me.

Publication date: Sunday, October 04, 2009

Will somebody pick up the phone?

When the phone rings at my house, my family has a ritual response. My husband ignores it.

I ignore my husband ignoring it.

And my son comes running toward both of us, frantically waving the receiver in his hand, saying "I don't know who it is."

In my day, we had a solution to this mystery. We called it, "Hello?"

But these days, we have Caller Identification, which can obviate the need to be polite to your friends and family when you have a sink full of dishes, a stove full of simmering pots or a body full of lethargy. What would we do with our friends were we not so good at systemically ignoring them?

Of course, disregarding your intimates is not the reason we have Caller ID. We have it to ward off the intemperate telemarketers, politicians, robo-callers and assorted assailers of domestic tranquility who have taken to the phone lines to insist that there is, despite our best efforts to discount it, an Outside World that always wants a piece of us.

Now it seems that Caller ID is flawed. Well, not flawed, exactly, just as porous as the rest of technology. The New York Times reports that Caller ID is backfiring. Consumer advocates say the equivalent of phone hackers have been monkeying with Caller ID so that the number on your screen may be a series of zeroes, a no-name local number or a charitable organization. In fact, the real caller is some sneak from Nigeria who has landed in a hotel in Prague without his luggage, needs a few Euros to tide him over and is happy to accept your credit card number.

"You don't know who is on the other end of the line, no matter what your caller ID might say," Sandy Chalmers, a division manager at the Department of Agriculture, Trade and Consumer Protection in Wisconsin, told the newspaper.

In other words, you could be paying $9.95 a month for Caller It Isn't.

The best part about Caller ID spoofing may be that people begin answering their phones again, for the sheer curiosity of wondering who is at the other end. The worst part may be that it forces us to revert to our pre-Caller ID days of "screening" our calls through voice mail. That means returning home to a mass of beseeching voices, yammering "Hello? Hello? Look, I know you're there. Will you pick up the phone?"

I'm not sure what it is about phones that they have turned into our ultimate maternal totem. We're lost without them and we can't be bothered answering them.

It's communication on our terms or not at all.

I struggle to inculcate phone manners in my son, if only because most of his friends are either a.) Terrified of the phone; b.) Affixed to the phone; or c.) Loutish on the phone. "Yo," they say, 'Sup?' or better yet, "Speak," as if Rin Tin Tin were on the other line.

"Press the green button and say, 'Hello, this is Paul speaking," I drill.

"But what if I don't know who it is?" he says.

"But that's the whole point of answering the phone."

"It could be somebody bad," he says. Well, yeah, it could be the telemarketing stick-up man, but perhaps there is some value in teaching my son to divest us of these pollutants in a solicitous manner.

My mother had a good solution to these domestic nuisances.

"Don't answer it," she would say when the phone would ring just as she had flopped down on her chenille spread, a can of Tab slapped on her forehead and a Mary Renault novel waiting mid-thigh.

"But it could be important!" I would insist.

"That's why you shouldn't answer it," she would say.

This was in the day when the telephone had a Delphic prominence in the household, its stature designated by a pillar-like "telephone table," at which one would actually sit still and attend to the prattle from the other end of the receiver.

Like many people, my mother was of two minds about the phone. She was alternately hanging on its every whisper ("What was that? Was that the phone? Get it! Get it!") or dodging its incessant bleating. "Tell them I died and went to Bloomingdales," she would say.

"Mom!" I would say, balking at the lie. "I can't do that."

"OK, tell 'em it was Loehman's."

My mother was gender-specific about answering the phone. If it was a male, she'd rouse herself, and it was a female, well, it was the death by Bloomingdale's.

"Nobody ever answers the phone these days," she says now. "All I ever do is talk to your brothers' answering machines."

"Well," I say. "People are busy."

"Oh don't give me that," she says. "I was busy before busy was born. People don't want to talk to me. They're ignoring me."

"I can't imagine where they learned that," I say.
"Me neither," she says. "It's rude as hell."

Publication date: Sunday, December 18, 2012

It's The Little Things We Do Together

After Al and Tipper Gore's marriage imploded, I started worrying about the hedges.

The boxwood hedges that erratically fence our front lawn are the third rail in my 17-year marriage. Invoking them in conversation, strolling by them with a sharp implement, or merely plucking a hapless, pathetically misaligned leaf from them can be cause for a marital squabble whose venom exceeds all horticultural parameters of civility.

No doubt this quarrel speaks to some larger, more malignant fissure in our marriage, the depths of which I have no zest to uncover.

The fact is ours is a mixed marriage. I am a boxwood absolutist, reared in the tradition that boxwoods are to be slashed to geometric precision, their maverick nature to stick, creep and bloat curtailed. Boxwoods require discipline. They must be scrupulously hacked, sliced and chiseled to resemble their etymological progenitor, the box.

My husband, a '60s rebel, believes the boxwoods should be liberated to soar, swell and nurture with beer-barrel liberality. Let nature take them. And take them, and take them, spewing out on to the street like insulating foam, their feral branches cascading in forsythia-like languor out on to the street.

Our intransigence on this agricultural point makes the Arab-Israeli conflict look like the 13th-century meeting of St. Francis and St. Claire in Assisi. The agreement is this: I take care of the hedges on the right side of the front yard. He takes (naturally) the left side.

But what I have feared of late is this: Is this what finally sent Al and Tipper over the (h)edge? Was it just one too many electric hedge trimmers assaulting the rhododendron? One too many stray toenails in the Percales? Was it just, "I don't care if you won the Nobel Peace Prize, if I have to tell you to lower the seat one more time, I'm going to flush you back to Oslo."

Among all married couples, I suspect, there is this unspoken, yet deeply held pact: "Once we get past 20 years, we get to coast." Nobody says it, naturally, but secretly we all make a little deal with ourselves: I won't say anything about that extra chin you have, if you don't mention that the last time I was a size 6 was during the Reagan Administration. I'll say nothing while you grow a rump the size of an ottoman if you don't rib me about my penchant for flannel pajamas and Ben & Jerry's Chunky Monkey.

This is called the Too Lazy to Try Anymore Concordat, and the Gores abrogated it, making the rest of us vulnerable to the big "D." The sundering of the Gores' marriage resembled nothing so much as the Christie Brinkley divorce. What kind of a man could not be satisfied with Christie Brinkley? (A pervert, as it turned out, which was no consolation). The whole thing makes you feel as if the future of the comfort waist band itself is under attack.

Not long ago, the father of a friend of mine, a long-married patriarch, well into his 70s, came into the family dining room and announced, "I've been unhappy my whole married life. My time to start living is now."

A cynic might say it was a little late, or that he had an

unmitigated nerve to call his entire family life fraudulent. But many couples are following his lead. The Boomer generation, with its creed of continual self-actualization, is particularly apt to divorce. Some experts say more than one-third of divorces occur in couples who have been married for more than a quarter century.

"Mostly it's people in their late 50s and early 60s," Phyllis Bossin, a Cincinnati, Ohio, lawyer and past president of the Family Law Section of the American Bar Association, told the Providence Journal. "Being 60 is a lot younger than it used to be. If you're a baby boomer, you're young when you're 60. People think, 'I've got 30 years left. I can have a whole other life.'"

If 40 is the new 30 or 60 is the new 50, then wither the 40-year marriage? Any historian can tell you that the 40-year marriage, to say nothing of the 48-year-old nursing mother, is a new twist in human history. Historically, men went through several wives, and not because they "grew apart," but because childbirth, disease or backbreaking labor killed them first. As marriage has grown longer, we have also asked more of it, as historian Stephanie Coontz has reminded us.

"For thousands of years, love, passion and marriage were considered a rare and usually undesirable combination," Coontz has written, adding that the Roman Catholic Church initially saw Valentine's Day "as a check on sexual passion."

"Even though young people centuries later turned the holiday into an occasion to celebrate romantic love and sexual attraction, few of them expected to marry on the basis of such irrational emotions. Almost no one believed that falling in love was a great and glorious thing that should lead to marriage, or that marriage was a place to achieve sexual fulfillment."

So those of us who are hoping for the soul-mate who will read us Browning as we lay dying, are the hopeless cockeyed-optimists worthy of a Rodgers and Hammerstein musical. You can pity us or you can praise us. We are the crusaders of a Brave New World, a realization so invigorating it can make you want to hurdle the boxwoods.

Publication date: Sunday, June 13, 2010

That is, like, so random

Every generation has its expression. For Baby Boomers, it was "cool." For my generation, it was "Whatever." For Generation X, it was "dude," and for my son's generation, the word is "random."

Everything that my son and his friends find unusual, weird, out of the ordinary or just plain funny, they label as "random," as in, "Dude, that is so random."

Acclimating myself to this idiom has not been easy. I was just getting used to "Whatever," as in, "I'm like, whatever, about the English language."

Moreover, I came of age in the "Man" generation, as in "Man, that is wild."

Every time I hear myself referred to as "Dude" (and yes, people do), I get a sudden urge to surf.

The use of "dude" to refer to both males and females seems so, well, random, as my son would say, or "like, so totally wrong."

The only word in my son's lexicon that I hear more than "random" is the word "epic," as in, "Dude, that was an epic Gladiator dodgeball game."

Now, when I hear "epic," I tend to think of Gilgamesh, or Odysseus. I think of Aeneas, Dante or Milton. In a pinch, I might include D.W. Griffith or Cecil B. DeMille. I do not think of dodgeball, homework or car rides to the Cape as especially epic, but then I'm from the generation that brought you the television miniseries.

What I find peculiar about my son's use of the word "random" is that his seems the least random generation in history. No kid worth his Crocs strolls over to the home of another kid and casually — randomly — asks him if he wants to come out and play. These assignations must be prepared several months in advance, slotted into a Blackberry and clocked to the one-hundredth of a second. Not too long ago, I tested this theory. I brought my son and a basketball over to a friend's house, rang the door bell and was confronted by a flummoxed mother.

"We're just wondering if Jack wants to play," I said, dribbling the ball on her step.

"What, you mean, like now?" she said, as if I had asked, "We were just wondering if we could have Jack's left eyeball."

My son set me straight.

"When you were a kid," my son explained to me recently, "you could like run out your back door and go ask some other kid to play. Now, if you did that, the person would be like, 'What the—?'"

The whole luxuriant sea of arbitrariness that marked my childhood has now been replaced by a Microsoft Excel program. Spontaneity is the lead paint of 21st-century childhood. It must be effaced with an ammonium sulfate solution of day camps, music lessons, martial arts class, algebraic tutorials and horseback riding seminars. Otherwise, your children risk emotional impairment and you could face an epic lawsuit.

My son is a kid in love with his imagination, which means that he spends a lot of time anthropomorphizing little plastic figurines, creating Byzantine charts on scraps of paper and covering sheaf after sheaf of recycled paper with images of penguins (Don't ask).

I begin to wonder if my son's recurrent use of the word "random" might have a deeper meaning. Could he be employing "random" not to describe the world he lives in but the world he wants to live in? Could, "That is so random" suggest that not a shred of his life is open to serendipity? Could it mean that every diversion that he dutifully marches off to is one more reminder of the suppression of his generation's caprice? Could it mean that he and his cohorts feel lashed to their refrigerator schedules in the same way their parents are leashed to their Blackberries?

Or could it be just, like, totally random?

Publication date: Sunday, June 26, 2011

Powering past their parents

In the fourth grade, I gave an oral report on Nigeria to my class. It was called "The Land and People of Nigeria," a title cribbed from the slender, Pop Tart-sized book with a khaki cover and a series of black-and-white maps.

I took notes from the book and penciled them onto 3-by-5-inch index cards. In the right-hand corner of every card, I wrote the page on which I had found the information. In the left, I scribbled the author's initials and the first three letters of the book's title. No one in my busy house would listen to my great oration about the vast plains along the Jos Plateau or the coastal swamps that snuggled along the Gulf of Guinea. So, on a Sunday afternoon, I stood in a corner of my grandmother's kitchen and recited the whole report to her.

"That's marvelous, darlin'," she said. "Come over here and lemme give you a Devil Dog." And as I sat across from her, inhaling the crumbly brown cake with its lather of vanilla frosting, I was light-headed with the thought that I had taught my grandmother something. I had illuminated the world. I told her about the non-fiction section of the library, which included maps with raised mountain elevations, and light blue rivers the same color as the varicose veins that creased our neighbor Mrs. Collins' thighs.

"It must be wonderful to have all that information at your fingertips," my grandmother marveled, and took out the plastic Michigan Rummy game. "How about a game?" she'd ask. I'd shuffle the deck, she'd pull out her cigar box of pennies and I would feel like the smartest, luckiest kid in Greater Boston.

Now in the fourth grade, my son is working on a PowerPoint presentation on South Carolina.

He brings me to the computer and thumps the tip of his index finger along the keyboard. His fingernails are long and caked with half-moons of dirt and I am resisting every maternal urge to haul him into the bathroom and scrub his nails down to his cuticles until I realize that this is his chance to teach me something.

I have no idea how to do a PowerPoint presentation. My son is going to show me. He is 10. I'm not sure how to take this.

"Pick a topic, Mommy," P.J. says, and I opt for Thomas Lawrence, a 19th-century British painter about whom I have recently written. I'm hopeful that this selection will designate me as a person with a modicum of intelligence, and not just some mutton-head who cannot even muster a PowerPoint presentation.

With a manual dexterity that no hunt-and-pecker has any right to possess, P.J. calls up pages and special effects, manipulating my words so that they scramble, fade in, dissolve and swipe across the screen. I suggest we might use pictures and tell him that I
have such pictures at work and that if we wait until after the weekend, perhaps he will teach me to insert them.

No need. P.J. clicks on the Internet and, in a flash, Lawrence portraits materialize, are copied, magnified, shrunk, and placed on pages faster than you can say "Copyright Infringement."

"Can we do this?" I say, the murky legitimacy of the Internet's free-for-all weighing heavily on my conscience.

"We do it at school all the time," he says.

Wonderful, I think.

"Mommy, you do it," he says. "Go to 'Effects' and scroll down to the one you want."

I blow it on the first try.

"It's OK, Mommy," he says. "Try again."

In about as much time as it takes to say "Sponge Bob Square Pants," P.J. and I have generated a serviceable, if legally dubious, PowerPoint presentation about a British painter nobody in the fourth grade has any right to know about.

We watch the PowerPoint presentation over and over again on the computer screen and I stare at P.J. with a mixture of amazement and fear. My son has already eclipsed me, I think, and it will not be long now before I have exhausted my reservoir of wisdom. I think about my grandmother, Nigeria and the Devil Dogs. I wonder if what I told her about the Niger River and British colonization had any real meaning for her, or if what really mesmerized her was watching me stand there in my Danskin shirt and Levi's jeans, swaying foot-to-foot and trying to pronounce "Yoruba."

I discover, not long after, that without P.J. I am maladroit to the point of hopelessness in creating PowerPoint presentations. It seems I learned nothing at all from what my son has taught me — except, perhaps, about a mother's susceptibility to awe, which can arrest even the reflex to scrub her little boy's fingernails.

Publication date: Sunday, September 25, 2011

Heeding a Mother's SOS

When my mother called a little after 10 on a Friday morning, her message was succinct: Tracey, I need you. Come now.

"Now" is a nettlesome term when 130 miles separates you from your mother. But my mother doesn't issue summonses frequently or with this much gravity, so I stuffed a few jeans and turtlenecks in a gym bag and sped up I-84 east, toward Boston, toward home.

Never mind that home now is a tidy lemon cape on a cul-de-sac in Connecticut, which I share with a husband, son and affectionate hound. Yet, in the atlas that houses my internal compass, home is always north. Home is always where my mother is.

Three days before my mother's directive, she had undergone back surgery at Newton-Wellesley Hospital. Details of the procedure were murky. My mother either knew and didn't want to alarm me or, more likely, didn't really know and just wanted the whole thing done. "Forget the facts; just fix me," would have been a reasonable edict that someone like my mother would issue a neurosurgeon.

But within 24 hours of her discharge, my mother was in a realm of pain she had never imagined. Hence, the mayday, issued to anyone within a 200-mile radius that shared her genetic code. Driving along the familiar ribbon of interstate that connected us, my apprehension ballooned. My mother had always been unsinkable, with a titanium-strong drive and dauntless resilience that could make those half her age feel like slugs.

Her age, I thought uneasily. Because my mother bore me at 19, I had always considered her young. But last November, she turned 70, celebrating her birthday as she always did, with a performance in a nightclub in Boston's Back Bay. We were all there, her children and the posse of fans my mother had collected in more than 35 years as a nightclub singer. She was gimpy but in full voice that night.

It made me recall so many nights with her, closing down cocktail lounges and nightclubs all along suburban Boston. I would be exhausted and exasperated, dragging my mother's microphone stand and a travel bag of clanging props back to the parking lot, where her pine green Pinto beckoned. Up went the hatchback. Clang went the cymbals. Thud went the enormous Fender amplifier my mother hauled into the back, like a longshoreman heaving bales of cotton. I'd spear the microphone stand through to the back seat and we'd be off on the smooth gray asphalt of Route 128, my mother rationalizing the choices she had made in her life as the tires murmured sibilantly beneath us and I struggled to stay awake.

What I remember most about those rambling, expansive monologues was my mother's endless struggle to balance her need to perform with her desire to raise three children. Talent, I learned early, was not a gift. It was a burden. It itched away at my mother and prodded her, pushed her away from us and left her with a fulfillment always tempered by guilt. Applause is addictive. But it is never as sustaining as a child's hug. She knew that. And it shamed her.

"You don't owe me anything," I remember her telling

me once. "Get that through your head. I can take care of myself."

But no one can take care of themselves all the time. No one should. We are connected through filaments of love and obligation, need and desire. And some of that love means understanding that the ones you need most also have needs of their own that need tending. Today, when we talk about mothers balancing work and family, I think about those women who have gifts that can distance them from the ones they love – writers, artists, musicians, composers. I think about the choice their children have to make, calibrating their needs against the urgency of their parents' creative impulse. My mother wouldn't have been satisfied with the church choir. That didn't diminish her as a mother; it enlarged my understanding of what love is, of what it must indulge and sometimes overlook.

"Hey, I'm better than when I called you," said my mother, as I open the door to her apartment. She is sitting in her Lanz nightie in a pair of knock-off Uggs, a tray of medications between her and HGTV's "Love It or List It."

She wagged her cell phone at me. "Can you believe I'm getting phone calls for gigs?" she said, laughing.

For the next two days, I cleaned her floors, washed her windows, made and laundered her bed linen and fetched her oatmeal and chicken broth from the market. I endured more television than I have in the last 20 years and just when I thought I solved the puzzle on "Wheel of Fortune," my mother said, "You can go now."

And I do. And she thanks me. And she tells me I really didn't have to do all that I did. But I know that I needed to do all of it and more. My mother is not old yet. But she will be. And I want to be ready.

Publication Date: February 17, 2013

Is Google Really Making Us Stupid?

A few days ago, my son asked me if the computer knew everything.

That was my fault.

I had become lazy in trying to answer the diverse and outlandish questions 7-year-old boys are apt to pose. I consider myself a reasonably well-educated person, but knowing the length of the red-ruff lemur's tail is quite beyond my scope. So when these questions arose, I generally did what we all do when some Delphic mystery confounds us: I Googled it.

The perils of this approach were obvious — my son would begin to imagine, as he demonstrated, that the computer was one giant brain, an infallible, omniscient force of unimpeachable accuracy. The dangers of this were obvious.

First, I don't want to be replaced. Second, allowing a 7-year-old to type every mite of cognitive marginalia into Google's search engine makes him vulnerable to the Internet's seemingly inexhaustible supply of smut.

But beyond all of this, was my very real fear that resorting to the Internet to attend to every passing curiosity would make my son an intellectual slug.

This month, the cover story of *The Atlantic* asks, "Is Google Making Us Stupid?" a reasonable question given the pervasiveness of the Internet and the intractability of stupidity. In the *Atlantic* story, writer Nicholas Carr worries that the Internet's accessibility and speed has changed the way he thinks. It has made him an impatient and truculent reader, an avid skimmer of words and an edgy and intolerant fact-grazer: "Immersing myself in a book or a lengthy article used to be easy," Carr writes. "My mind would get caught up in the narrative or the turns of the argument, and I'd spend hours strolling through long stretches of prose."

Now, he says, the Internet is "chipping away my capacity for concentration and contemplation. My mind now expects to take in information the way the Net distributes it: in a swiftly moving stream of particles. Once I was a scuba diver in the sea of words. Now I zip along the surface like a guy on a Jet Ski."

Carr doesn't actually answer his question, though he offers up a lot of anecdotal evidence that Google is, apparently, making us dumber.

At least one study from University College, London, has found that people using popular research sites employed a form of "skimming activity," jumping from one source to another like bees in a flower garden, sucking up information and storing it, while moving on to the next blossom. The Internet, according to one developmental psychologist, puts a primacy on "efficiency" and "immediacy," thereby weakening our capacity for deeper, more engaged reading. (And, one supposes, putting subscriptions to The Atlantic seriously at risk.)

The *Atlantic* article coincided with my ill-fated attempt to read *Stuart Little* to my son. The E.B. White story captured my imagination as a girl, providing years of intrepid and provocative dreams. But my son reacted listlessly. The words, Stuart's priggish diction, and the overall pacing of the story seemed sententious and inflated to P.J.

As a kid, I had read Stuart's donnish delivery as clever. It's not every day you find a mouse who talks like Ronald Colman. But P.J. didn't get it. He yawned, he pawed through the book, looking for the next illustration. Finally, he just asked me to quit.

"Don't you want to find out if Stuart finds Margalo, honey?" I asked.

"It's just not interesting to me," he said.

I had found the same response to *The Hardy Boys*, *The Wind in the Willows*, and even, to a certain extent, *Alice in Wonderland*. These classics were positively antique to my son, their idioms foreign, their syntax strained. It was like having a *People* magazine subscriber read Joseph Addison's *Spectator*. The stories he liked — *Geronimo Stilton*, *The Magic Tree House* and (gulp) *Captain Underpants*, moved briskly. Illustrations cluttered the text, and, in the case of "Geronimo Stilton," they were the text. They're clever, they're visual and, most of all, they're fast.

When my son asks me if the computer knows every-thing, I reply that it does not, but that the encyclopedia does. We have two sets of them and, though a few items may be outdated, they are more than adequate for researching, say, J.M.W. Turner, or even red-ruff lemurs. And so we yank the dusty Britannica out of the oak book-case, slap it on the bed and begin thumbing through the onion-skin pages.

And then, of course, as it is with dictionaries, so, too, with encyclopedias, and we become distracted by this or that entry, landing here and there and filling our own gray matter hard drives with all sorts of marvelous ephemera.

"This is fun," says P.J., and I nod in agreement, remembering when I was 7 and the encyclopedia knew everything, and all I needed was my mother to guide me as we searched together, the magic of learning.

Publication date: Sunday, July 13, 2008

The Tracker Made Me Do It

I am being led into temptation. Stalked by the demon of materialism. Ads are following me.

Specifically, shoe ads.

A comfortable, dowdy pair of Rockports tramps behind every website I visit. "C'mon," it seems to whisper. "You know you want me."

Well, of course I do, but I was aiming for fiscal prudence.

That's becoming increasingly difficult as advertisers become more manipulative, consumers more vulnerable and willpower as obsolete as typewriter ribbon.

The stalking shoes are a type of marketing called "retargeting," in which online retailers track what you perused online and then pester you with reminders to buy the very items you dismissed. Retailers like Zappos, B & H Photo and the Discovery Channel already use these kinds of ads, the New York Times reports. But with Google and Microsoft entering the field, retargeting has become more pervasive — and resisting temptation more challenging than ever.

In fact, retargeting has becomes so invasive that the Federal Trade Commission is considering "Do Not Track" legislation that would allow Internet users the ability to control whether advertisers can track their online behavior and browsing history.

And, as any shopper knows, nothing quite helps the

resistance of temptation like legislative prohibition.

In *We Have Met the Enemy: Self-Control in an Age of Excess*, Daniel Akst argues that contemporary society has lost its self-control. The obesity epidemic, the financial crisis, addiction to everything from sex to shopping to the Internet, and a savings rate that, until the financial implosion, was in the negative digits have collaborated to making willpower one of the qualities most envied and least employed.

"A lot of the behavior we call addiction is really a love of pleasure that carries the force of habit," he writes. Reframing our personality failures as "addiction," he argues, absolves us from blame.

We lost self-restraint, he asserts, when the fundamental pillars of society that checked our impulses — community, hierarchy, church, family — began to crumble.

In their place, as author Barbara Ehrenreich has powerfully argued, is the proliferation of the you-deserve-it Gospel preached by celebrities like Oprah, which insists that acquisition is not only what we need to sooth our perturbed spirits, but what we deserve.

Throw into this toxic stew increasingly sophisticated marketing techniques like shadow ads and you've got a brew against which self-control stands little chance.

"There is research that shows people still have the same self-control as in decades past, but we are bombarded more and more with temptation," Kathleen Vohs, a professor of marketing at the Carlson School of Management told The New York Times. "Our psychological system is not set up to deal with all the potential immediate gratification."

Odysseus famously had his sailors lash him to a mast to avoid the tantalizing sirens. Think what such inhibition might have done for Brett Favre or Tiger Woods. In principle, Odysseus' realization that he was vulnerable to temptation, is what underlines mechanisms like 401ks and Christmas Clubs — put the money away before you see it.

In 2011, downsizing household debt is the top financial goal for consumers, according to a recent online survey from the National Foundation for Credit Counseling. It's a laudable goal in a country nearly undone by debt.

But it's going to take a lot of willpower to walk away from a tempting pair of shoes that keep winking at me with such devilish allure.

Publication date: Sunday, January 30, 2011

Meet our new receptionist, Kitty

In the late 1980s I worked for a company whose receptionist was a blue-eyed blonde with the wide vowels and clipped consonants of a John Cheever housewife.

Julie wore Lily Pulitzer skirts, Pappagallo flats and satin headbands from Talbots. She was trim, tanned and tactful and filled out light pink While You Were Out slips in glorious Palmer penmanship. Though she had grown up in upstate New York, the daughter of a sheriff, Julie had the look of a Miss Porter's graduate who spent weekends at the Cosmo club. Every morning, she would fold a copy of the Washington Post into a tidy rectangle and time herself on the daily crossword, which she completed between answering phone calls. On a good day, she's have the puzzle solved by 10 a.m.

Julie was, in other words, a low-paid, high-class, under-employed intellectual who answered phones, filed expense reports and changed the coffee filter from 9 a.m. to 3 p.m. daily. Once upon a time, there were a lot of Julies, gracious, considerate sophisticates who welcomed you to the office every morning, inquiring about your weekend and complimenting you on your attire.

Today, we have "Hello Kitty."

Hello Kitty is one of the new robotic receptionists "employed" by a Japanese company that charges $424 a month to ask visitors to speak their names and tell them when the person they want to see is ready for them. Hello Kitty has 20,000 stored conversation patterns, including songs and riddles.

Then there's ALICE, a "virtual receptionist" manufactured by a Las Vegas company that is based on an interactive, touchscreen video panel much like the one you use to withdraw funds from your ATM. "When a customer walks into an ALICE-equipped business, motion sensors alert the company's employees, who can then turn on their video capabilities and answer the client's questions," reports the Las Vegas Review Journal.

Or there's the $10,000 QB Robot by Anybots Inc., a free-standing mobile robot that, the Boston Globe reports, many companies are using as a receptionist. Ava the robot (not to be confused with EVA the robot from "Wall-E"), is a 5-foot-4 assistant whose "head" is an iPad or Android tablet, which moves via motion sensors. Eventually, Ava could progress beyond receptionist to nurse maid or cocktail waitress, dispensing pills or fetching cocktails, the New York Times reports.

"I like the idea that if you have a party, the robot can recognize faces, take drink orders, go back to the kitchen, load it up and then go back and find those people and deliver the drinks," Colin M. Angle, the chief executive of the iRobot Corporation, told the Times. "I think that would be awesome."

Awesome? Is this really what we want from our interactions? Do we want an actual personal connection, the warmth of a stranger's smile, the polished courtesy of a human on the other side of a desk, or do we want a transaction?

Increasingly, businesses are deciding that what we want is a transaction. The Globe reports that many startup companies are relinquishing receptionists, reasoning that they look more frugal if they forgo the cost of a human and replace it with an informal, kiosk-like greeter. "In the start-up world," one architect told the newspaper, "you don't want to look like you're wasting money."

In March, David Brancaccio of NPR's Marketplace, reported on a trip he took across the country with a goal of having no human interaction whatsoever. Accompanied by four GPS devices, a robotic dog named Wilson and the robotic radio station Pandora, he slipped into Hyatt hotels via the hotel chain's kiosk, never having to deal with a human for 3,200 miles. By the time he reached Tucumcari, N.M., he reported, he was "finding the interaction unfulfilling. "It ain't living," he wrote. "We talk about the personal connections enabled by texting, skyping, social media. But is this really where we're headed as technology increasingly invades all business and personal relationships?"

It may be. Increasingly, I find myself gravitating to the self-checkout aisle at the local grocery store, if only because by the end of the day I am often too tetchy to face another human being and I foolishly reason that I can check myself out faster than a done-in grocery clerk. It's not an impulse I admire in myself, but society is making it easier for us malcontents to evade human contact entirely. So extensive do many organizations believe this misanthropy extends that many Internet organizations do not even employ people to answer their phones. And good luck if you can actually find the number that bypass the phone tree maze.

So, I think about Julie the receptionist often when I visit offices that have all the warmth of a fallout shelter. I think of her gentle welcome, mollifying me as I stormed into the office, her judicious inquiries reminding me that the world did not revolve around my travails. Mostly, she showed me that a gentle smile and a warm reception could actually change the texture of my day, a change that I dare any robot to duplicate.

Publication Date: August 19, 2012

Talking Seals fill the Gap

Meet Paro. Paro may be your mother's new best friend. Paro is a devilishly cute stuffed baby harp seal that purrs when petted, looks up adoringly at its handler and brightens at the sound of its name.

Paro is also a robot with a $6,000 price tag and may do more for your aging mother than you have the time or inclination to.

One of a flock of new "sociable robots," already in widespread use in Japan to support seniors, Paro is a sign of things to come and a symptom of a widespread malady: our tendency to relegate human intimacy to the realm of technology.

"Paro is the beginning," Sherry Turkle, director of the MIT Initiative on Technology and Self, told The New York Times. "It's allowing us to say, 'A robot makes sense in this situation.' But does it really? And then what? What about a robot that reads to your kid? A robot you tell your troubles to? Who among us will eventually be deserving enough to deserve people?"

In her fascinating but disturbing new book, "Alone Together: Why We Expect More from Technology and Less from Each Other," Turkle provides some answers to that question, and they are chilling. It is not just that we are sloughing off our responsibilities to the aged to a bunch of fuzzy Tamagotchis, it is the alarming realization that by the time Generation Y gets to their rocking-chair days, they might consider a wooly empathy machine the best cure for what ails them.

Take Anne, a mid-20s graduate student who told Turkle that she would trade her boyfriend in "for a sophisticated Japanese robot" if the robot evinced "caring behavior."

"If the robot could provide the environment, I would be happy to help produce the illusion that there is somebody really with me," she said. Who needs all those squishy, leaking carbon-based need-machines called people when the arms of fiber optics beckon?

"I'd rather talk to a robot," one 30-year-old man told Turkle. "Friends can be exhausting. The robot will always be there for me. And whenever I'm done, I can walk away."

USA Today labeled 2010 "The Year We Stopped Talking to One Another," in part because it has become so staggeringly apparent that people would rather type, Tweet or text than talk. Although more than 90 percent of us have cell phones, two-thirds of teens say they are more likely to text their friends than call them, a Pew Research study found.

As one 35-year-old woman told *The New York Times*, "The only reason I ever call someone anymore is if I don't have their Twitter handle or e-mail address."

For more and more of us, the boundary between the virtual world and the physical world has eroded completely. We might thank technology for what it reveals about what we really want: to control our identity and repel any intrusion into our intimate space. When E.M. Forster articulated the need to "only connect," the emphasis was on *connect*. Now it is on *only*.

"Technology is seductive when what it offers meets our human vulnerabilities," Turkle writes. "As it turns out, we are very vulnerable indeed. We are lonely but fearful of intimacy. Digital connections and the sociable robot may offer the illusion of companionship without the demands of friendship. Our networked life allows us to hide from each other, even as we are tethered to each other."

Turkle's book is most moving when she turns to how children are affected by their parents' frenetic addiction to their electronic gadgets.

The "ping" or "bleat" or chime of an electronic device is like some other, more appealing-but-demanding sibling whose needs supersede their own. Children are not stupid. They know when they are being abandoned, even if what they are abandoned for is a piece of technology no bigger than a rattle.

Undivided attention — the familiar and disarming look from a cherished friend — the silence between words in which so much is expressed, is fast becoming an obsolete artifact of a vanishing world.

It is in those moments, of course, in which our truest self is revealed and in which we become most authentically who we are.

To purge such an intrinsic element of our identity in the name of efficiency is a form of social suicide, whether we realize it or not.

Then, only our plush-pal robots will be able to console us.

Publication date: Sunday, March 27, 2011

Ambushed By The Gas Pump

I am watching television at the pump. I want to watch television while I am pumping gas about as much as I want to drink the gas spewing from the pump, but I have been ensnared. My captor is Gas Station TV, which discharges 4 1/2 to 5 minutes of visual effluent to hapless drivers who have stopped into one of the 12,000 gas stations in the country that "broadcast" its infernal prattle.

Gas Station TV is one more moth hole in the increasingly permeable membrane that separates private citizens from the insidious advertising industry.

It "transforms the gas station to a highly sought-after media destination to inform and influence consumers at a desirable Point-of-Purchase, when they are mobile and can be influenced to take action at a nearby retailer in proximity," according to its publicists.

In other words, you've been ambushed at the gas station by an advertiser masquerading as a weather report. The only obstacle between you and that bag of Cool Ranch Doritos is eight baby steps and $1.89.

Now, nobody's going to nominate Gas Station TV for an Emmy, but you have to admire the ingenuity of the idea. With technologies like TiVo, DVR and the felicitous mute button, advertisers have had to do a lot of ducking and weaving to be heard.

But anybody who has taken to the open road in pursuit

of a little silence can easily feel ambushed. Screens —
in the doctor's office, at the bank, at the airport, in the
convenience store, at the checkout corner and — lest we
forget — in your home, have become the wallpaper of
contemporary living. But unlike the benevolently mum
wallpaper, these screens are talking, moving, bleating and
otherwise niggling at your increasingly shattered brain
cells.

This Orwellian nightmare is called "place-based media
space." The idea is that nobody stays still anymore. And
even when they do, they have the indecorous habit of
muzzling commercials, which has the effect of flushing
advertising dollars down the toilet. So advertisers have to
get you where you live — on your cell phone, at the gas
pump, at Wal-Mart and in all those parenthetical places
where you used to be able to try to get your head together.

You are not alone if you feel besieged by these ubiqui-
tous screens. The average American household has three
televisions, two DVD players, one desktop computer and
two cell phones. We spend, on average 4.5 hours watching TV a day — that's more than we spend on any other
leisure activity. The Kaiser Family Foundation reports
that children 8 to 18 years spend nearly four hours a day
in front of a TV screen and almost two additional hours
on the computer and playing video games.

So what do you do when you have a nation full of
brain-numbed video junkies? Jack them up with more
junk.

I cannot imagine who on earth wants to be transfixed by a television screen while weighing their seedless
California grapes at the grocery store. While I can appreciate that a little aggravation sets in while you're standing
six-deep in the express check-out line, that's what those
cheesy tabloids are for.

Similarly, I am sure that the well-intentioned executives at the bank merely want their customers to be well informed, but it can make a person queasy cashing a check while watching a CNN report on GIs blown to smithereens in Afghanistan.

I suspect these irksome additions are supposed to take customers' minds off of the fact that they're waiting, which has become some sort of crime against humanity. But nothing expands the frustration of waiting than the flatulence of wall-to-wall TV. If all Hell breaks loose in the universe, I'm sure I'll get a big clue-in when I get home and can turn the television on —or off— at my leisure.

Publication date: Sunday, September 06, 2009

Don't Worry, be Happy

A confession: For most of my life I have harbored a deep and abiding suspicion: It pays to be shallow.

While many of my more cerebral pals might deride an acquaintance as a worthless flibbertigibbet, I think: I wish I could be like that.

"Gawd," they would say, "That woman is a chowder head. Did you ever meet anyone who talked so much and said so little?"

"Terrible," I'd say. But I silently churn with ambition toward frivolity. How much better it would be to prattle on about pillow swatches, *American Idol* and the Kardashians than to fret over Original Sin or theodicy. Never again to be paralyzed by my stubbornly brooding nature.

Wouldn't it be better to cluck merrily over *The Real Housewives of Atlanta*, mambo along with *Dancing With the Stars*? The unconsidered life seemed not only well worth living, but so much less burdensome. Who needs to slog through my melancholic mire? Happy people, it turns out.

Researchers from the University of Arizona have found that people who spend their day having deep discussions and less time engaging in small talk seem to be happier. "By engaging in meaningful conversations, we manage to impose meaning on an otherwise pretty chaotic world," Dr. Matthias Mehl, author of the study, told the

New York Times.

According to Dr. Mehl, even if your attempts to find meaning fall flat — you've consumed an entire chicken Caesar salad and still can't understand how a divine Creator could let annihilation despoil the earth — you're still going to be happier. Why? Researchers suggest it's because you've got somebody across the table as flummoxed as you.

But at least you talked. And at least you had someone to talk to, which, researchers say, is critical in the pursuit of happiness.

Researchers have been telling us a great deal about happiness these days, belying those cynics who carp that all these eggheads whittle away their time in worthless abstractions. Bah! Very Smart People have been spending buckets full of research dollars investigating critical issues like what makes us happy. Most of that research has concluded that pretty much everyone has a "set point" for happiness, suggesting that the chronically miserable are virtually certain to stay that way, so you should stop wasting your time telling them to buck up.

One of them those researchers is George Vaillant, director of a 72-year-old study of 268 men who entered Harvard in the late 1930s. Vaillant has pretty much decided that what makes us happy is not what happens to us, but how we respond to it. Resilience is infinitely superior to a Powerball payout, which experts assure us makes no one happier, and this is why we continue to spend millions trying to disprove their thesis.

Some researchers, like Mihaly Csikszentmihalyi of Claremont Graduate University in California, suggest people are often clueless about what will make them happy.

For instance, people at work generally believe they'd be happier at home, only to return to their burrow, where they are miserable, irritable and bored.

In fact, group activities tend to help our happiness levels, Csikszentmihalyi asserts, even if you're a sloth like me and spend most of the time moaning about not wanting to go anywhere but your own den. If you must bellyache, it is best to do so with another grouch in a public place, preferably while smiling.

Recent research found that those who smile a lot are usually happier, have more stable personalities, healthier marriages, better cognitive and interpersonal skills.

That is more than enough to make you hate them, but if you want to be happy, you should resist the temptation and grin up a storm. In a place like Connecticut, which at least one study suggests is among the least happy in the country, we can use all the smiles we can get.

Publication date: Sunday, November 21, 2010

What We Keep Is Who We Are

My husband is a pack rat, a keeper of stray sea shells and ticket stubs, smooth, palm-sized rocks from the Outer Banks and bottle caps with unusual logos.

I am a purger, a trash-heaver, a scourer, a hurler of all ephemera, no matter how sentimentally invested. This makes me a ruthless and cynical cleaner, and no doubt adds a little kick to my marriage, but I am unlikely to change and neither is my husband. We are both mulishly convinced of the virtue of our domestic hygiene—or lack thereof.

But of course, there are limits. And there are contradictions.

And those we will leave to our 12-year-old son to sort out someday.

One of the most tempting places for a wannabe ascetic like me is the Container Store, which gives the illusion that the solution for our blizzard of acquisition and sentimentality is more drawers. If we could only just find a place for all our doo-dads, we'd absolve ourselves from possessing too much junk, and save ourselves from the horrifying realization that we just incinerated our son's first sketch of his hand. It's why more than 11 million American households rent storage space, a more than 90 percent increase since 1995.

But there are some things we cannot jettison. What

we keep bears directly on who we are.

Ten years ago, when my grandmother died, and my brothers and I sullenly prowled through her closets and attic, feeling both intrusive and madly curious, I realized how most of what we keep lies somewhere between worthless and ridiculous.

My grandmother had costume jewelry and polyester pant suits. She kept used wrapping paper and flattened ribbon. She had chenille bedspreads and plastic mules. She had knick-knacks of terriers and little shepherd boys. She had coffee tins filled with rolled pennies and memo pads cinched with pink rubber bands. She had nothing, in other words, that would mark her as anything other than a very frugal old lady. Out of all of the debris — and in the end most of what we keep is little more than that— that clotted her house, the one treasure I took was this: A letter-sized envelope on the back of which was written, "Frank— let the dog out."

Frank was my grandfather, a barrel-chested, hazel-eyed Irish immigrant who I knew largely as a severe old man with mitt-like hands who spent the last decade of his life tethered to an enormous oxygen tank. He worked nights at a Raytheon plant off of Route 2 in Lexington, Mass., and so it would have been natural for my grandmother to remind him to take the dog out when he came in. Natural and gorgeously ordinary.

In a recent New Yorker article, Pulitzer Prize winner Jhumpa Lahiri wrote of the paucity of printed works in her childhood. It was not, she later realized, the acquisition of books that she craved but, she wrote, "a better marked trail of my parents' intellectual lives: bound and printed evidence of what they'd read, what had inspired and shaped their minds."

"Frank — let the dog out."

Of all of the rubbish in my home that I so ruthlessly junk, somehow I can never part with that scrap of paper. It sits in a wine case that holds evidence of still more of my inconsistencies as an ascetic: my grandmother's letters to me. A few springs ago, the letters were damaged in a flood that gurgled up through our basement. They are black with mold now and will likely worsen over time. I cannot throw them out because they hold the part of my grandmother that escaped the fate of the trash bin—the ceramic Thumper, the Hallmark plaques, the $2 picture frames and laminate furniture.

"I am writing this letter at 4 a.m. before Danny goes to work," she wrote me, referring to my uncle. "Auntie Ruthie told the funniest joke last week at cards. Let me see if I can remember it for you." My grandmother would ramble on with the joke, always forgetting the punch line and then enclose a pack of stamps, aware that money was tight for me, keen on never wanting to lose the thread of my life.

I can never imagine being as enigmatic to my son and his children as my grandmother was to me. But eventually, all of the material accretions of my life will pass on to them. My books, of course, will yield erratic but considerable truths. My emails and tweets will thankfully vanish into the cyber-ether. But my letters, and those of my grandmother, will yield the richest fruit, reminding them that the most authentic fibers of our lives are contained in the words we commit to paper, the elegant and the ordinary, merging on the page to remind us of who we are.

Publication date: Sunday, July 10, 2011

Pride and Shame, or
The Wealth of Poverty

My grandparents were poor. They were not shack-poor. They did not make clothes out of flour sacks or stews out of root vegetables. They did not beg on the streets or live out of their rusted, powder blue Ford LTD. But Nana and Grandpa Pascarella lived in rented housing all of their lives, until they grew very old and moved to subsidized housing.

"The projects," was what Grandpa called the dwarfish red brick apartments into which he stuffed their possessions, a few heavy cherry dressers handed down from my great-grandmother and a vinyl recliner held together with duct tape.

My grandfather was a laborer all his life and had broad, leathery hands in which he used to crush shelled walnuts and cool roasted chestnuts. I used to trace the lines in his honey-colored palms with my small fingers as I sat with him in his recliner, where he taught me magic tricks. "Look at this," he would say to me, his index finger tracing the indentations of my cuticles. "Just like mine, see? Think we're related?"

I laughed because I was fair and light-eyed and my grandfather turned the russet red of an old barn every summer. For most of my life, I had no idea what he did, although I knew he could lay carpet like nobody in the business and could wash a floor so it glistened. He taught me how to wash a floor, really wash one, he said, with a scrub brush in one hand and a soft cloth in the other. "In my family, everybody cooked and everybody washed," said Grandpa, who had grown up one of 12 children of two Italian immigrants in East Boston. As a boy, he used to steal coal from the coal yard, a sin for which he asked forgiveness at the Mission Church. "What could I do, Father? My family is freezing."

When he was bad in school, which was often, he told me, winking, the nuns used to give him a "rat hand," slashing him on the fingertips with a bamboo swatch that had been soaked in vinegar. Grandpa was a southpaw and whenever he wrote with his left hand, he got a "rat hand," a memory that could make him wince 60 years later.

Grandpa taught me card tricks, because he was a card player but, mostly, he went in for the horses. He'd place $2 bets at Suffolk Downs with my Uncle Frank, a man who wasn't my uncle and who seemed never to lose. Uncle Frank had a few bucks, Grandpa liked to say. "But that bastard wins every time."

Grandpa never won, just like he never had a few bucks. He was sly and clever and nimble and he dashed from job to job for a few extra cents in hourly wages. He told me often of the houses he almost bought, or should have bought, or had a chance to buy. He took me by them sometimes in his Ford LTD, which we used to wash together on Sundays. "Could have had that one for $8,000. Can you believe it?" he'd say, tilting his fedora toward a cozy cape.

"Why didn't you, Grandpa?" I would say.

"Huh," he would chortle and clack his teeth together. "What a question. What a question."

The difference between my maternal, Italian

grandparents and my paternal, Irish ones, was stark. To the Pascarellas, my Irish grandmother was rich, which was not true, but must have seemed that way to them, when my brothers and I charged into the house on Christmas Eve, loaded down with boxes, bags and packages we had acquired at her house.

All these years later, I wish I could erase the memory of my Nana's face as we muscled by her with our booty, stuffing it under the tree and boasting of our good fortune. It was the look of someone trumped, outdistanced, bereft. I tried to act blasé, to soften the blow to Nana, who sat impassively in a colonial-pattered armchair, smoking Salems and looking askance at my mother, trying to preserve her battered pride.

"Got lucky, huh?" Grandpa would say, his lips a little pursed.

When my Nana had snuffed out her Salem and we had taken our places around the tree, she would look at me and say, "You know your Nana gets you things you need." I looked up at her, aware of the unspoken clause "and all that she can afford." "Yes, Nana, I know," I would say, mustering a nearly physical gratitude. "I really appreciate it. Really."

It is not within the power of a child to assuage the anguish of parents or grandparents too poor to give. No assurance, however earnest, can persuade them that they have failed this critical test of their affection. What could I have done to assure my Nana that the gifts, so out of reach for her, never mattered, that all I wanted was the whoosh of cold air she created when she arrived in the doorway in her lamb's wool coat, redolent of Estee perfume, my grandfather, his fedora cocked, following mirthfully behind?

It is not within the power of a child, but it is their

penance, to recall their own inability to soothe the broken hearts of family whose impoverishment was petty and whose wealth was more than they knew.

Publication date: Sunday, December 25, 2011

For shame, for shame

In *Silk Parachute*, a collection of personal essays, John McPhee tells of a letter his mother wrote him while he was in college in which she used the word "shame" 44 times. The catalyst for this galling-gun shaming was an all-night poker game that McPhee told his mother he'd taken part in. She saw the poker game as decadent and shiftless.

Regardless of one's views of gambling, it seems as doubtful today that a mother would lambaste a college student with a machine-gun like invocation of shame as that she would pen a letter and actually put it in a mail-box. Shame, like hand-written letters, is an artifact of a more genteel age.

Or maybe not.

The advent of YouTube, as what one writer called our visual pillory, has reacquainted us with shame, though with peculiar results.

Last year, an English bank worker who was caught on tape flinging a tabby cat into the garbage bin, had her life turned upside down after a video of the cat-disposal was posted on social media sites. Although she was fined $400 for cat-battering, Mary Bale has also received death threats. Nobody puts Tabby in the trash bin.

Social media, reports The New York Times, "is the new court of public opinion. With the freedom to post just about anything online, sites like Facebook and Twitter are making it easier to shame people whose behavior might otherwise remain unknown or slip by unnoticed."

And yet one wonders: Does anyone's behavior really go unnoticed today? In George Orwell's dystopian novel "1984," Big Brother was the collective state prying into the lives of its citizens. Today, Big Brother is a self-appointed militia of camera phones fanatically chronicling every blip of behavior and rushing to post the best bits online. What shocks us now is not when an incriminating video is posted online — and viewed ad infinitum by those with nothing to do — but when aberrant behavior is not caught on video.

Late last year, when the newspaper for which I toil reported on allegations of police brutality by a group of young Waterbury adults, I cannot have been the only one in the Brass City thinking, "What? No video?"

It's tempting to wonder whether the ubiquity of video cameras will incline us toward better public behavior. It's doubtful. This is, after all, a society in which we require posted prompts to remind us to wash our hands after using the toilet (which, leaving nothing to chance, is automatically flushed for us).

Take, for example, the edifying MTV series *Teen Mom*. Here is a "reality" show in which the participants, including Amber Portwood, are only too aware of the blanket of cameras that swaddle their lives. How, then, to explain the September episode in which Portwood was caught on tape slapping and punching Gary Shirley, sometimes in the presence of their daughter, Leah? Portwood now faces three counts of battery and one of neglect in Madison County, Ind., reports the *Herald Bulletin*.

Leave aside for a moment that *Teen Mom* has been declared a "breakout hit" for MTV. Leave aside the

inversion of our usual understanding of domestic violence as a male batterer thrashing a woman. Leave aside,
too, our evidently obsolete concept of "family" or the fact
that "teen motherhood" is so normal that we accept it as
TV fodder. Can a woman, aware of the ogling eyes of an
ever-present camera, beat the stuffing out of the father of
her child on tape and experience anything near to shame?

Sadly, we have so lost the understanding of this ancient
check on behavior that many have grown immune to it.
While some may see these videos as our new gallows for
public humiliation, some of the participants see them as
platforms for smug indignation. Why, for instance, would
the perpetrators of the malicious behavior at Iraq's Abu
Ghraib prison memorialize their offenses on video. Why
would a U.S. Naval officer — an officer — produce salacious videos to be picked apart in the inevitable autopsy
of his military career?

But we cannot be surprised. In a world where a path-
ological blabbermouth like WikiLeaks founder Julian
Assange nets a publishing deal worth a reported $1.7
million, shame itself has been taken by the scruff of the
neck and plunged into the dustbin.

Publication date: Sunday, January 09, 2011

We Need More Civility – Now!

Not long ago, I drove into a traffic snarl just outside the local Catholic school. I had mis-timed my commute and a swarm of harried parents were orbiting around the school's drop-off point. As I approached the church's exit lane, a woman in an SUV began to accelerate into the oncoming traffic, which, in this case, consisted of me. I could see the back of the woman's head and a cell phone plastered to her ear as she looked the other way and pulled into the main street. I punched my horn, alerting her to our imminent collision.

She looked in my direction, hit the gas pedal and flipped me the bird.

Heaven help us if she learned *that* in parochial school.

In its audacity and veniality, the incident was disappointingly routine. Just another 21st century commute, navigating the shoals of intemperate drivers with more cylinders than sense.

But in its audacity and excess, it underlined one of the critical shifts in the erosion of civility. Even when we are demonstrably in the wrong, our default position is to attack. When a stranger censors, the best defense is an aggressive offense, the more vulgar the better.

The co-founder of Johns Hopkins University's Civility Initiative insists civility among Americans is plummeting, a view confirmed by a majority of Americans, according to a PEW Charitable Foundation poll. "We are both ruder and more civil than it times gone by," Pier M. Forni told *The New York Times*.

But that, of course, depends on what you mean by "times gone by." In the 16th century, one ate with one's hands, usually from a common bowl, picked one's teeth at the dinner table and, long into the 19th century, customarily shared a hotel bed with a stranger. As late as 1832, Frances Trollope complained of the "incessant, remorseless spitting of Americans," and personal hygiene was, at best, indifferent.

When people talk about the demise of civility, they generally mean the deterioration of manners from the early-to-mid-20th century among a certain social class. Advances in living standards – more square-feet per home, more cars per garage, and more appliances per capita – are insignificant if not accompanied by improvements in social behavior. Does it matter whether you can fit 5,000 songs on your iPod if you can't get along with your next-door neighbor?

For most of history, technical advancement initiated social improvements – scientific advances led to increases in disposable income, which led to higher levels of personal conduct. But in the 21st century we have developed an inverse relationship between technological advances and social customs. The more avenues we have for communication – cell phones, e-mail, Facebook, Twitter, texting, YouTube – the worse we seem to be at it. It may be that the plethora of social networking has led us to look at society as just another slice of spam to be deleted.

Judith Martin, a.k.a. "Miss Manners" has noted that when we complain about the loss of civility, what we mean is that we expect people to be more civil to us, and not necessarily the other way around. Increasingly, researchers have begun to calculate the costs of perceived incivility in how it affects, for instance, our performance at work.

In *The Cost of Bad Behavior* by Christine Pearson, the Arizona management professor discovered that incivility was rampant in the workplace and that most, or 60 percent, of that rudeness came from above. This, too, is a shift. It used to be that those of higher income and rank were recognizable for their courtesy; now they are distinctive for their boorishness. In Pearson's survey, half of the 9,000 managers and workers she surveyed said they decreased their performance on the job as a result of the rudeness. It is a paradox, she said, of contemporary management: Managers expect their employees to treat their customers with respect, while employing very little of it on their own.

When my father died of a massive heart attack six years ago, my brother was working for a prominent financial service firm in Boston. Not one of his hundreds of co-workers showed up to my father's funeral, nor did they send condolences to my brother. Within a month, my brother left the firm for a lower-paying job.

It was not, he said, that he wanted to punish his colleagues, merely that he did not want to spend so many of his waking hours with people who had no heart.

And that, of course, is the whole point of civility. It is not surprising that after Joan Didion's husband died, the most obliging words of comfort were supplied by Emily Post, as she wrote in *The Year of Magical Thinking*.

Etiquette proceeds from the notion that we view others as moral, vulnerable beings, worth of our consolation and respect. That is the real lubricant of a social network that we dismiss at our peril.

Unpublished

When Too Much is Just Too Much

Two women saddled with shopping bags walk past a newspaper box. The headline blares "Americans Not Saving Enough."

In the cartoon, by Steve Kelley of the *New Orleans Times-Picayune*, one woman turns to the other and says, "That's ridiculous. I bought four pairs of shoes and saved $60."

Welcome to the 21st century's idea of thrift.

After years of being told to spend our way out of the economic cellar, we're now being encouraged to squirrel away our princely salaries to re-energize the economy.

The country's consumer debt is at a record high while its savings rate is at a 25-year-low. That has turned financial analysts from the pages of The *Wall Street Journal* to *USA Today* frantic with pleas for austerity. "Somebody had better get loud about this in a hurry," said Dan Houston, senior vice president of the Principal Financial Group. "So many Americans have let (saving for retirement) slip, replacing it with plasma television, new cars and houses two-thirds bigger than what we need."

But in today's a penny-saved-is-a-dollar-splurged economy, want and need have become inseparable. In part, that's because what we want has become a poor substitute for what we really need.

So argues Peter C. Whybrow, a neuroscientist who

puts the U.S. on the shrink's couch in *American Mania: When More Is Not Enough*. Whybrow says Americans have equated the pursuit of happiness with the pursuit of material wealth. He says we've already achieved what might have been labeled happiness and are now in a ravenously acquisitive territory beyond. Americans are, he says, not only the wealthiest country in history but the only civilization to achieve the widest distribution of wealth among its citizenry. "Never before in the history of our species have so many enjoyed so much."

"Species" is the operative word for Whybrow, who is a scientist, not a sociologist. He argues that the abundant wealth and plethora of choice in America "has fostered an acquisitive behavior in America that (is) now testing the limits of our ancestral biology... In short, in our compulsive drive for more, we are making ourselves sick."

American Mania is part of an expanding array of thumb-suckers by self-appointed deep-thinkers like Gregg Easterbrook and Barry Schwartz, that try to unravel this contemporary conundrum: If life has gotten so much better, why do we all feel so much worse? In works like *The Paradox of Choice* and *The Progress Paradox: How Life Gets Better While People Feel Worse*, Schwartz and Easterbrook explore just how good life has become and just how darn miserable people, stubbornly, insist on being.

Easterbrook, a senior editor at *The New Republic*, tries the badgering nanny approach, maintaining that life has become appreciably better for the middle class and that if we don't buck up and get happy, the whole world could starve to death.

Schwartz is a bit more empathetic, asserting that being offered 32 different types of toothpaste is not liberating, but emotionally exhausting and intellectually dishonest. (If there are 225 channels, but only two are worth watching can that be classified as choice?)

Into this fray walks psychiatrist Peter Whybrow, informing us that all this cupidity has rewired our brains and made us insatiable, manic and perpetually, defiantly, unhappy. Incidences of anxiety have doubled in 10 years. Depression is increasing, particularly in the young. The demand for wealth, he writes, has created "an accelerated, competitive lifestyle that steals away sleep and kindles anxiety, threatening the intimate social webs that sustain family and community.

For many Americans the hallowed search for happiness has been hijacked by a discomforting and frenzied activity."

Whybrow says this is because we're biologically wired to enjoy consumption. Consumption activates the neurotransmitter dopamine, which electrifies the brain's pleasure center. What stops us from acquiring everything in sight is very much the same brake that stops us from scarfing down all the tiramisu at the birthday party: social embarrassment.

But with a 24-hour buying center via the Internet, and a decreasing concern about what our neighbor thinks, we're gorging on the buffet bar, spiraling into debt and astonished that we, as the old Alka-Seltzer commercial said, ate the whole thing. Whybrow argues the bottomless appetite for things substitutes for what we really want, which is relationships with others.

"Neurobiology teaches us that we're reward-driven creatures on the one side, which is great," he told The New York Times. "It's a fun part of life. But we also love each other and we want to be tied together in a social context."

Whybrow insists that we've overloaded circuits and become gluttonous lab rats, stuffing ourselves with pellets when what we really want is a little chat with the rat next door.

So the next time you're ready to dash to the latest shoe sale, stop by and gab with your neighbor.

Publication date: Sunday, May 08, 2005

Money Doesn't Buy Happiness – Until it Does

Ask Americans which they'd rather be: richer, thinner, smarter and younger, and you pretty well get the result you'd imagine. Being rich trumps pretty much everything. Immortality is useless without the bling.

Implicit in the desire to be rich is the certainty that it guarantees happiness. We all like to tell ourselves that this is not true, even while we anxiously upgrade from analog to digital, cell phone to Blackberry, DVD to Blu-Ray, Walkman to iPod. Just another upgrade, a few more gigabytes, and a smidgen more megapixels and happiness will follow.

About a third of Americans say they're happy, and about half say they're pretty happy, according to the Pew Research Center. A recent study found that people became happier as their income grew, but the effect leveled off at about $75,000 annually — which gives us all something to shoot for.

But something's wrong. Mathematically, we should be a heck of a lot happier than we were 30 years ago because the average per capita income in the U.S. has more than doubled since then. Yet, our happiness index hasn't budged.

It could be we're victims of the "hedonic treadmill."

As defined by psychologists Philip Brickman and

Donald Campbell in 1971, the hedonic treadmill theory stipulates that people respond only briefly to financial ups and downs but ultimately revert to their usual state. So, the first time you open that iPod Classic you get a juicy squirt of happiness that lasts maybe as long as a stick of Big Red chewing gum. But pretty soon, you look at your scratched-up old iPod Classic and start wondering if maybe you should spring for an iPod Touch. Or maybe, for a few dollars more, an iPod Classic.

Perhaps it's not your gigabytes that need upgrading. It's your definition of happiness that needs to be tweaked.

In "Exploring Happiness: From Aristotle to Brain Science," Sissela Bok examines the nature of happiness from the minds of philosophers, writers and religious figures. The book looks at how these thinkers defined, and presumably achieved, lasting happiness.

For centuries, the word "virtue" was inextricably linked to happiness — and happiness, all agreed, was the ultimate goal of humankind. A happy man (and let's face it, men were the only ones allowed the luxury of such ruminations) was the virtuous man. Or, as Aristotle put it, "the happy person is the one who expresses complete virtue in his activities." Happiness, as many have said, is "the well-being that consists in well-doing."

When these guys said "Life is Good," they might have added, "only when you are."

Stoics like Epictetus and Seneca, went further. For them, happiness depended on our ability to suppress our sensuous appetites. You'll be happy if you strip yourself of avarice and recognize that one gigabyte more or less does not ecstasy ensure. You're probably better off with a transistor radio. Or maybe, nothing at all! For the Stoics, hedonism and consumerism were not only dishonorable, they didn't get you anywhere.

Today, of course, the satisfaction of sensual pleasure is at the root of our definition of happiness — and our economic system. Virtue has not only been bled out of the definition of happiness, it's acquired a prudish veneer. Virtue is not the wellspring of happiness, but its scourge. The man of virtue is a wet blanket, a Gloomy Gus, a prig, a bore! Happiness is the Rat Pack, baby! It's an "Oceans 11" orgy with Beyoncé bumping and grinding her billion-dollar booty in Prada. It's Lady Gaga descending into a room full of celebrities in Alexander McQueen.

It's that bliss when you're lying on the beach in Cozumel, sipping a Dewar's on the rocks, musing, "There are some things money can't buy. For everything else, there's MasterCard."

For the 21st-century American, materialism has supplanted virtue as the lynchpin of happiness, greased by the country's $276 billion advertising industry. That explains why we spend more money on shoes, jewelry and watches than we do for higher education. As a culture, we're not getting any younger, or thinner, or, heaven knows, richer. But we could get a little smarter. And we might start with a better definition of what it means to be happy.

Publication date: Sunday, September 19, 2010

Emergency Preparedness Drill

Two days after a howling snowstorm that thundered mercilessly through Connecticut just before Halloween, I walked my dog through the inky black thicket that our neighborhood had become.

Trees, pendulous and shared, lay strewn across the street like Tinker Toys. More still seemed imperiled, their sheered branches hanging from trunks by strands of meaty fiber, like a tender root of a child's loose tooth. All along the narrow cul de sac on which we walked, power lines dangled like pythons from shredded limbs. No streetlights illuminated our path. No candles glinted from windows. I held a headlight I had stripped from my bicycle, which shed a silvery glow into the silky dark.

Somewhere, a generator purred tantalizingly and I realized how unprepared I was for disaster.

Disaster is relative, of course. I had not been felled by a tree. My roof had not caved in on me. Neither my health nor that of my family was endangered. Over the days that followed, when the state looked as if it had been unilaterally, if unevenly, clear cut, plunged into collective darkness, I thought about the meaning of words like disaster and devastation, alternately empathizing with those without power and feeling the terms a little hyperbolic.

Certainly, there was a difference between devastation and inconvenience. Surely, a distinction could be made between irritation and desolation.

In the five days that we were without power, my small family huddled around a bayberry-scented candle we received for Christmas, feasting on the cobbled together perishables we could rustle up from the refrigerator. We ran our hands under cold water and swathed ourselves in a collection of sweaters, afghans and winter coats. If we were feeling hearty, we would last until 6:30, whereupon, vanquished and weary, we would blow out the candle and head for bed.

I am a suburban kid whose idea of roughing it is staying at a hotel that lacks a fitness facility. I do not do well with axes, camp grills, hand-saws and battery illumination. I am not proud of these limitations, but neither have I done much to remedy them. It seemed a perfectly acceptable deficit.

Until the pre-Halloween snow storm lashed through the state, turning the idea of Trick or Treat into an episode of *Survivor*, I had looked at my home like most 21st century Americans. It was an investment, a place to decorate, serve guests, impress family. But in the days that followed, I noticed my own priorities turned more elemental.

I had an almost atavistic hunger for a hot meal. I yearned for the consoling heat of a hot shower. I worried about the state of my roof and the viability of my shingles. My husband and I, drawn together by affinity and romance, began to look at one another as helpmates. We trudged through the jungle of twisted limbs, twigs, rust-colored oak leaves and slices of gutter, and began to prioritize the demanding physical labor that needed to be done. The two of us took hacksaws to the weary old oak and sawed numbly away. We hauled branches the size of fruit trees into the wetlands behind our house and I found myself wishing, for the first and hopefully last time in my life, for a pet ox.

In the cold, dark days that continued, I began to look at my home on a more basic level. It was shelter. It was that "roof over your head" for which my father always told me to be grateful, and which I had never fully appreciated. It was that place that kept us from being victims of the violent gunfire-like popping of limbs and thundering of tree trunks that kept us awake on the evening of the snowstorm. I had never lived before in a federally designated disaster area. But there was something in having endured it that readjusted my priorities, and, even if temporarily, shifted the relationship I have with my home.

It was a refuge, a hearth, a place that embraced my family and the peril that lay just outside our door.

Publication date: Friday, November 11, 2011

Couldn't She Write about 'Nice' People?

In the summer of 1955, after the publication of her seminal collection of short stories, "A Good Man Is Hard to Find," Flannery O'Connor received a fan letter from a clerk working in a credit bureau in Atlanta. The clerk had taken issue with The New Yorker's negative review of O'Connor's book and asked O'Connor whether these stories were really "about God."

As insights go, this one was not especially keen. Since the publication of *Wise Blood*, which O'Connor later described as a "comic novel about a Christian malgré lui," the Georgia author had been labeled as a Catholic writer, writing with a confrontational brutality many readers found unendurable. Her misfits, murderers, perverts and pious Christians were forever pulverized under her castigating, and often self-righteous, glare. Why was O'Connor so cruel to characters who so patently needed redemption? Couldn't she, as her imperious mother pleaded with the publisher Robert Giroux, write about "nice people?"

What the Atlanta clerk, Betty Hester, identified was O'Connor's scorching conviction that there really were not "nice" people, only the saved and the damned. O'Connor's stories relentlessly flay conscience toward often imperfect revelation. Weighty, weird, wondrous and cruelly ironic, O'Connor's fiction may have been the last gasp of a literature that engaged with the supernatural world.

A new, workman-like biography of O'Connor, "Flannery: A Life," by Brad Gooch (Little, Brown and Company, $30) has been published and it is long overdue.

What it reminds us of is not just the searing prose and daring parables of this Southern Catholic writer. It also reveals the paucity of good literature that is fearless in its use of religious allegory.

The biggest rise in publishing in the past few years has been the increase in spiritual /religious books, although the line between spirituality and self-help tends to be too slender for my taste. O'Connor would have recoiled at any moniker other than "writer," but she wrote with a cudgel-like insistence on morality and grace. If that meant that a simple doctor's visit by a good Christian woman could result in that woman being set upon by a stranger, lunging at her throat and calling her an "old warthog from hell," so be it. As O'Connor said, "Grace changes us and change is painful."

O'Connor's acid sense of humor, which often derived from clueless characters oblivious to the overwhelming promise made to them, leavened her stories with mirth that seemed a little naughty for a devout Catholic.

Although I first discovered O'Connor in a high school anthology, it wasn't until I was in my early 20s, living alone in a rented room in the eastern part of Connecticut, that I appreciated the emphatic ferocity of her faith. Violence might be the opposite of grace, but O'Connor was unafraid to use it as a vehicle. That marvelous line that the Misfit utters after he has just murdered an imploring grandmother, "She would have been a good woman if there had been somebody there to shoot her every minute of her life" — could pretty much suit all of us.

O'Connor, who didn't own a television until a congregation of nuns gave her one in 1961, said she wrote these gothic stories to shock a morally blind world. As she said, "To the hard of hearing you shout and for the almost blind you draw large and startling figures."

Most of O'Connor's stories were written in the 1950s, those halcyon days of peace and good manners to which many would willingly return. It's harrowing to conjecture what she would have made of the more apocalyptic drone of today's violence — the Columbine shootings, the Virginia Tech slaughter, the Wesleyan murder — or the annihilative tendencies of ex-lovers who blow away those they professed to love.

In 1960, she wrote, "We live now in an age which doubts both fact and value, which is swept this way and that by momentary convictions." As a writer, O'Connor was on a quest for the "redemptive act," the shattering act of horror that gives humanity "the chance to be restored."

At the end of her life, she asked for prayers to send her "the kind of grace that deepens perception."

In 1964, O'Connor died of lupus, the disease that had claimed her father. She was 38. Her book, *Everything That Rises Must Converge*, a line drawn from one of her heroes, Pierre Teilhard de Chardin, was published posthumously.

Most of what passes for "spiritual/religious" literature today is the warmed over, feel-good goulash of the Gospel of Oprah, offering such banalities as: God wants me to be happy; God wants me to be self-actualized; and, my favorite, God wants me to be rich.

O'Connor brooked no truck with such bunk. She suggested that what God wants is for me to make a decision.

"The stories are hard but they are hard because there is nothing harder or less sentimental than Christian realism," she said once about the violence in her work. "When I see these stories described as horror stories I am always amused because the reviewer always has hold of the wrong horror."

Publication date: Sunday, May 31, 2009

Making Light of the Good Book

The problem with the Bible, as we all know, is it's just too darned long.

What would make the Good Book even better is an abridged version. Better yet, an annotated version, by a person deeply steeped in theology — a person like, say, Jane Fonda.

Jane Fonda tells me that Jesus was the first feminist, a revelation that might be inspiring if it had been delivered by a more theologically creditable source.

As it is, it's overly simplistic and reliably flaky.

Anybody who's read the Gospels — and has even the most passing interest in Jewish society of the first century — couldn't help but notice that Jesus spends an uncommon amount of time talking to women.

Whether that makes him a feminist or a person for whom women were in equal need of enlightenment is arguable.

Of course, the problem is that most people haven't read the Gospels, or read them well, so a gaggle of windbags from "Entertainment Tonight" are taking on Ecclesiastics today.

Religion is now the hottest category in publishing, Business Week reports. About half of all adults say they read at least one Christian book in the past year, Barna Research Group reports. "This is a significant shift in consumer interest," said Albert N. Greco of the Book Industry Study Group. Last year, the country bought 270 million "religious books."

But what is a "Christian" book? Is it Antonio Monda's *Do You Believe? Conversations on God and Religion*, in which sages like Spike Lee, Jane Fonda and Jonathan Franzen answer religion's most fundamental question: Does God exist? Or is it the *Left Behind* series by Jerry Jenkins and Tim LaHaye, which has sold 70 million copies by scaring people to death — or the nearest baptismal font? In 2006, Joel Osteen's *Your Best Life* Now, sold 500,000 copies. Is Rick Warren's *The Purpose-Driven Life,* which has sold more than 22 million, a Christian book? Or is it a self-help book?

What about the "Pocket Canons," individual, palm-size paperbacks of the Bible's books, introduced by some theological or literary celebrity, like (I kid you not) Bono? Does it matter?

After all, in a country in which we change religions with all the deliberation with which we change cable providers, isn't the mere reading of something, anything spiritual, better than trolling the Emperor's Club or text-messaging your girlfriend from the mayor's office? Does it help the agnostic to have Bono tell them that David was "the Elvis of the Bible?" Does it help the atheist to have Martin Scorsese — a man who has soaked the screen in blood and profanity — expatiate the book of "Job"?

Probably. Still, it's reasonable to question what special channel Spike Lee has to the Infinite, or what makes Jonathan Franzen think he's Reinhold Niebuhr.

The problem, of course, is that nobody knows Reinhold Niebuhr, whereas everybody at Easter dinner could probably name Spike Lee or Jane Fonda. Celebrities are our theologians today, sermonizing on everything from

Buddhism to body piercing. Most of them all come back to the same squishily vacant spiritual center, which has about as much theological rigor as a Hostess SnowBall. That, alas, is right up the alley of today's spiritual seekers, many of whom want ecstatic happiness, bodily perfection and Warren Buffett's bank account — all prepackaged in a tidy "spirituality" gift bag. For them, the Good Book is O, the Oprah magazine.

"What my students long for is not salvation after they die but happiness, here and now," Boston University professor Stephen Prothero wrote in *USA Today* earlier this year. "They want to discover themselves and to give voice to their discoveries. They want to experience joy because of their bodies, not despite them. And they don't want to be told what to do with those bodies, or with whom."

As Boston College's Alan Wolfe points out, the best-selling books in Christian bookstores are diet books like *What Would Jesus Eat?* and *Slim for Him*. A few years ago, Bruce Wilkinson released *The Prayer of Jabez*, which went on to sell 9 million copies. Jabez's prayer asks God's help in the accumulation of material wealth, a bit of marginalia that must have been excised from my Bible.

Narcissism with hymnals, in other words.

One of the reasons I love Holy Week, which ends today with Easter Sunday, is its grinding reminder that Jesus isn't a solution to suffering, but a participant in it. The problem I see with much of pop religiosity is its lust for an ecstatic experience, devoid of the contemplative rigor that is the meat of religious devotion — Easter without the Garden of Gethsemane.

What people are looking for in these books, it seems to me, is Salvation Lite, a new brand of indulgence that absolves them from the gnarly edicts of an imperious God. Well, perhaps He is exacting. Look around. Perhaps we need a little more of that.

Instead of trying to apologize for religion's exigencies, perhaps religious leaders would do well to find the liberation in them. In discipline there is enormous love. Or as C.S. Lewis—a real Christian writer—put it, "The hardness of God is kinder than the softness of men, and his compulsion is our liberation."

Now, there was a writer who made the Good Book worth reading.

Publication date: Sunday, March 23, 2008

Everybody Limbo

To hell with Limbo. Limbo, that murky little realm for unbaptized souls and folks who couldn't quite pass the entrance exam for heaven, has gone the way of indulgences.

The Catholic Church, which instituted Limbo during the Middle Ages to solve a theoretical riddle, is in the process of making a welcome, if belated, exit from the Catholic tradition.

It was never official church doctrine but had a meaty role for artists and writers whose imaginations were easily stoked by the concept of a place that ensured "natural happiness" that was nevertheless empty of communion with God.

According to several news reports, Pope Benedict XVI, never a big advocate of the theologically squishy concept, is ready to put the kibosh on Limbo, which he once dismissed as a "theological hypothesis." As Cardinal, the current pope shrugged off the concept, which St. Thomas Aquinas helped put in motion, as having "never been a definitive truth of the faith."

But for a time, Limbo solved a riddle of faith that St. Augustine had set in motion with his idea of original sin. What happens to all those babies who die before being baptized? which, to Augustine, was critical for salvation. It seemed harsh to condemn all those babies to hell merely because their parents hadn't gotten them to the baptismal font in time. By the Middle Ages, theologians had come up with a solution: Limbo was the neither/nor of the afterlife, a place where innocents would live forever in "natural happiness" without the communion of God.

Limbo is, in other words, the world in which many of us are now living.

Certainly many of my friends, devout secularists who ascribe to the creed of Sartre, or Seinfeld, the Dalai Lama or Homer Simpson, don't seem bothered by the murky ambivalence of Limbo.

After all, they're in good company. Dante confined all kinds of celebrated luminaries, including his own guide, Virgil, to Limbo, and they seemed none the worse for it.

What bothers them is not the lack of communion with God, but the forced communion with people who do believe in Him. Those are the people making life difficult for my secularist friends, forcing risible concepts like intelligent design down their throats or impeding the progress of science with their mulish objection to embryonic stem cell research and abortion.

But their objections to religion are mild compared to the vehement disdain for religion in the place that gave birth to Limbo, Europe.

Over the holidays, I received a phone call from my cousin Jane, in Britain. Jane lives in the north of England, not far from Leeds, the city that bred the terrorists who bombed London's train station last year. She is a devout secularist, of which there are many in Britain. As Karen Armstrong wrote in "The Spiral Staircase," World War II and Auschwitz mortally wounded faith in Europe, and it has gone downhill since.

Fewer than 7 percent of Britons attend church weekly. The Church of England has closed 1,700 churches since 1970, and continues to shutter about 30 churches yearly, reports The Washington Post. To many, like my cousin Jane, the church has become something worse than anachronistic. It has become a source of destruction.

"What has religion ever done for the world except encourage killing and hatred?" she said. "The Inquisition, the pogroms, the IRA. The jihads. Those Muslims in the subway. Those people in the plane. They hate you. Don't you see? They hate you and their religion tells them to hate you."

It was shattering to listening to this assault on faith. I couldn't fathom living in a world without faith, and Jane couldn't countenance living in a world with it. But both of us must navigate in a world in which religion is frequently invoked and exploited.

The worst, of course, are always "full of passionate intensity," but is it religious intensity? Or is it an ecstasy of another sort? In "The Death of Satan: How Americans Have Lost the Sense of Evil," Andrew Delbanco writes that the devil is always the seducer who most seems like the saint. Evil is evil because it cloaks itself so audaciously and effectively in good.

Behind my cousin's vehemence was a sense that religion had let her down. She wanted to believe in something she could no longer believe in. That, to my mind, is real Limbo.

Europe has lived with religion longer than we, and has borne the brunt of its excesses less charitably. It has cast its blame with religion as an instigator of mayhem, and very little will convince its citizens otherwise. Most of these countries are our allies, but their views of religion are dramatically different. While many of us look to religion for succor, our European brethren look at it with trepidation.

They are content to live in a state of natural happiness

without communion with God. To us, it is Limbo. But to them, it is liberating.

Publication date: Sunday, January 08, 2006

Heaven, I'm in Heaven

As a girl, I imagined heaven as a stairway on a median strip.

The stairs were made of an ethereal white substance somewhere between marshmallow fluff and dry ice. I imagined dancing up those steps a bit like the Nicholas Brothers in "Stormy Weather." I'd tip-tap my way between the grassy strip and the celestial heavens, where my great-grandfather sat on a piano bench, smoking a White Owl.

Heaven, in my childish view, looked like a collision between a family album and an MGM musical. People sang Harold Arlen songs, danced like Fred Astaire and sat around my great-grandfather's upright piano, talking about the quality of the corned beef.

I'm not sure when my concept of heaven shifted, but I will never forgive Cecil B. DeMille for derailing my Busby Berkeley-meets-Harry's Delicatessen view of paradise. After I saw *The Ten Commandments*, my opaque staircase evaporated. I could never think of Moses without picturing Charlton Heston and heaven lost all its pungency.

In a world in which fewer Americans profess a religious conviction, more than 80 percent believe in heaven, up from 72 percent in 1997. Of those, 71 percent believe heaven is an "actual place," according to a 2004 Gallup poll. Although not as many (71 percent) Americans believe in Hell, credence for both Hell and the Devil has grown over time.

In *Heaven: Our Enduring Fascination With The Afterlife*, *Newsweek* religion correspondent Lisa Miller tries to put some flesh around the scaffolding of heaven—not an easy task. The Book of Revelation details, with bejeweled precision, what heaven looks like, but ask most Americans what heaven looks like and it's a pretty hazy image. Of the three monotheistic religions, only the Qur'an describes with stunning specificity what heaven will be like — which may be why its fundamentalist practitioners are so hell-bent on getting there.

Perhaps because scriptural references are so ineffable, culture, in the writings of theologians and poets, has filled the gaps. Miller argues that Augustine and Dante — to say nothing of Albert Brooks and Alice Sebold — have had as much of an effect on our conception of heaven than early Christian fathers like Tertullian. Much of the Christmas-card imagery that clouds our perception of heaven was supplied by Renaissance masters like Giotto and Botticelli, who were both riffing off of Dante's *Paradiso*, published in 1321.

In *Heaven*, Lisa Miller goes on a quest to unlock what scholars and ordinary practitioners think Heaven is like. She is derailed along the way by her own obdurate rationalism, which can't grasp how God physically puts the pieces of mortal bodies back together in Heaven. "That's the one I can't do," she told me. "My rational mind can't do it."

"Reason," C.S. Lewis wrote, "is the natural order of truth, but imagination is the organ of meaning."

We are living now through a crisis of imagination, in which the ability to marvel, to wonder, to be drawn back in awe has been eclipsed by the empty promises of technology.

For many Christians, Heaven is a specific place, with people, food and, well, OK, perhaps even cigars, which they recognize and savor. My own belief in heaven has changed as my own faith has evolved. I believe that heaven is both here and not yet here. As Paul writes, it is a transfiguration that defies human understanding.

"For no eye has seen, no ear has heard, no mind conceived what God has prepared for those who love him," Paul writes in Corinthians. "Listen," he writes, "I will tell you a mystery! We will not all die, but we will all be changed, in a moment, in the twinkling of an eye, at the last trumpet."

So perhaps heaven is not a place we go, but a change we undergo. I hope it is a capacious place big enough to contain my piano-playing great-grandfather and small enough that I might bump into Lena Horne. "I'll build a stairway to paradise," Ira Gershwin wrote, "with a new step every day." I imagine myself ascending the steps like the Nicholas Brothers, executing fancy splits over Jane Austen and Fred Astaire. It certainly would be heaven for me to dance with the stars.

Publication Date April 5, 2010

Longing for the art of conversation

My friend wants to stop exchanging gifts.

It is too late this year, of course. By the time she proposes this moratorium, my meager package – a brown box stuffed with books, an ornament, misshapen Scottish shortbread – has already arrived at her door. I love to imagine her receiving the box, with its silly stickers and festive mailing label. I like the thought of her deliberately placing the wrapped gifts under her tree and waiting, as I know she will, until Christmas morning when she will unwrap them. I like to imagine her reaction – the sigh of recognition that comes when a friend has nourished the morsel of you that the two of you share.

But my friend frets over the time that I spend ferreting out this treasure and fusses, too, though she will not say it, over the money I spend. She cannot know the thrill it is for me to prepare my little package in New England and send it southward, knowing it will meet a receptive audience. She cannot know that she will rob me of that silly pleasure. We have come to an age, she says, where we don't need things to attest to our devotion, and maybe she is right.

All of this she tells me in a three-page letter that arrives a week before Christmas. The letter is on good, heavy paper and printed in a jolly red ink. The letter is newsy and discursive, toggling from the health scares of mutual friends, to the meagerness of our last shared salad, to a blunt criticism of a recently finished book that disappointed.

I read the letter at the end of the day, when I have purged my skin of the day's pollutants and plunged into a pair of fleece sweatpants and flannel top. I am very still when I read the letter, and alone, the only sound the sibilant spray of the shower in which my son sings softly to himself. It is one of those letters that can make you feel that you have dined with a person, looked into their familiar gaze and traced the pattern of their drifting thoughts. With a letter, of course, you have a souvenir. You needn't rely on memory alone.

A few days before my friend's request, I sat across from another friend I hadn't seen in two years in a coffee shop whose cheerful décor bled away as we spoke. His life has been hard and messy, and though there was nothing I could do to tidy the fraying of it, and though I brooded over it for days after, I felt strangely enriched. I realized how few genuinely attentive conversations I had had in the past year. I realized that it was not so much the talking I missed, as the listening.

The day after this friend left for home, I found myself ambling aimlessly in the local mall, needing nothing but looking for something. My gifts had been bought, wrapped and mailed. I had name tags filled out and receipts annotated, but still I dawdled, peering listlessly through the thick glass at the frantic shoppers, dodging parents clinging to the limbs of howling toddlers, picking up baubles and frippery and wondering what an overly disciplined shopper like me was doing in a mall four days before Christmas.

What I was looking for, of course, was a package that would give me the feeling I had when I left my friend at the coffee shop or when I sat transfixed by my friend's letter. I was looking to purchase the experience of conversation, of the charged energy generated by two people following one another's lovingly appreciated digressions. It's impossible to buy that, of course, which hadn't stopped me from trying.

The rampant debt with which so many of us are wrestling has been engendered in part by a gluttony for objects that substitute for the kind of experience I had with my friend. This year, as in many of the last, the most popular category of gifts was electronic gadgets, most of those relating to communication – Androids, Smart phones, tablets, net books. The irony is that all of these tools, meant to facilitate conversation, only obviate it. They make it easier for us to avoid one another.

I will miss the time I spent prowling about the bookstores and burning myself on oven racks – all part of the care I took to send my friend a gift I delighted myself in imagining that she would enjoy. But the gift of presence, the reward of intimate attention, is one that I long for most. All of the rest, I realize, was only a substitute for that.

Publication Date: December 23, 2012

Please get off the phone, please

Last month, Michigan authorities pulled a 45-year-old woman out of Lake Michigan after she fell off a pier while texting.

The plunge followed the plummet of a Reading, PA., teenager who tumbled into a mall fountain while she was texting. Meanwhile, in La Crescenta, Calif., a man texting his boss came face-to-snout with a bear walking up his staircase.

OMG.

I could have used a bear the other day while I was walking, and, I thought, conversing with a colleague in Waterbury. But a bleat from his Smart phone holster and my colleague was diverted – head down, thumbs fluttering, attention sidetracked, conversation terminated.

Doesn't anybody even say "excuse me" anymore?

It has become axiomatic in the 21st century that no conversation is without interruption. The only variable is what form the disruption will take. Increasingly, the intrusion is texting; more people now text than talk on their cell phones, a predilection more pronounced amid 18-to 24-year-olds than among 50-to 65-year olds. The old folks want to hear the intonation of your voice, the pauses between your clauses, the young folks want to control the message and check off their lists. While talking is generally something you have to do face-to-face – an *epic* psychological time suck – texting demands only a pair of thumbs and a fluency in emoticons.

"Texting and e-mail and posting let us present the self we want to be," writes Sherry Turkle, an M.I.T. professor and the author of "Alone Together: Why We Expect More From Technology and Less from Each Other." "This means we can edit. And if we wish to, we can delete."

And yet what strikes me about texting is that the very speed at which we receive and reply to a text has come to constitute a barometer of our deepest relationships. A friend of mine has a son, with whom she has had a volatile relationship. The relationship was so fractious, that my friend resisted visiting her son when he was in a serious bicycling accident. Instead, she inquired about his condition in a text message. "He texted me *right back*," my friend said, as if their testy relationship had suddenly been resolved. And yet I suspected the text was her son's way of avoiding a more emotionally exhausting conversation with his mother. He had done his duty and avoided becoming engaged. It was just the sort of interaction for which texts were designed.

"Here's the issue," Naomi Baron, an American University linguistics professor told The Washington Post, "We don't want to talk with each other most of the time."

Or, as one 26-year-old explained about her preference for texting her parents rather than calling them, "I put it off because there's something confrontational about someone calling you....You have to gear up for it."

Texting is the lingua franca of the teenage years, as anybody who has tried to talk to a teenager swiftly discovers. While a teenager can be verbally maladroit to the point of aphasia in conversation, when it comes to texting, he is a regular Anthony Trollope. Texting offers a control over our presentation of ourselves to others, just as it inures us from the spluttering idiocies to which we often fall prey.

As one 16-year-old boy told Turkle, "Someday, someday, but certainly not now, I'd like to learn to have a conversation."

I suspect that part of the reason we resort to texts is the same reason e-mail proved so valuable: It's expedient. You want a quick answer, a simple statement of fact —"arrived safely," — and you don't necessarily want to open yourself up to the ambiguity of a prolonged conversation. But how much of what we explore through conversation is fact, and how much of it is the groping elucidation of what we want to say, and an equally tentative understanding of what our partner is trying to get across?

I've made real blunders in conversation, and it can often seem that the more I try to undo them, the worse those faux pas become. But I've also been able to come to conclusions I would never have reached – not just about myself, but about my friends – had we not talked, ineptly, inexactly, until we have reached some kind of mutual insight.

"I just wanted to hear your voice," a friend of mine from California told me recently. "These texts only get you so far."

Yes, they do. But for some of us, that may be just the point.

Publication Date: June 12, 2012

Going Nowhere Fast

My friend has a kitchen drawer filled with travel articles.

They are places she would like to go, scraps and shards of pipe dreams. Corsica. Florence. Normandy. The Amalfi Coast. It has been years since she has begun collecting these articles, some of them frayed at the edges, shredded like hungrily torn morsels from a loaf of bread. I notice that some of the pieces cite prices in Greek drachmas and Irish pounds, and I hesitate to update her on the conversion to the Euro. This is her dream drawer, I conclude, the clippings set aside in the same way I dog-ear a page in a clothes catalog, never completely intending to purchase the circled item, but never really willing to dismiss the idea that I could.

My friend is at the age when members of her circle are beginning to retire and avail themselves of cruises and tours, the sort of deeply discounted, couple-centered excursions my friend dreams of taking. They return suntanned and hale, their arms full of boxes of Swiss chocolate or Irish linen, Florentine wallets and pistachios from Dubai. Over dinner they regale my friend with anecdotes and enthuse over the Caravaggio at the Uffizi, the Rembrandt at the Hermitage. They proffer their iPhones and, with their forefingers, page through photo after photo of white cliffs and cerulean seas, Corinthian columns and

Norwegian fjords.

My friend feels a longing she cannot articulate, a desire to consume all of these places in one glorious, TSA-free gulp. All of it looks so intoxicating and none of it looks attainable. She is an overworked professional, determined not to waste her life collecting clippings and fantasizing about places she will never see, waving goodbye and welcoming back, but never actually leaving port herself.

What is it about travel that is so intoxicating and yet so paralyzing. I look at the calendar and realize that I am suddenly 50 and by next year will have been married 20 years. I should do something to celebrate, I tell myself, go somewhere, take off while we're able, shoot the moon, blow caution to the wind.

But there is the roof to think about, the roof that is increasingly taking on the mien of a botanical garden and must be replaced. The house is peeling like a side of corn and needs to be painted or sided or attended to. Then there is the dog, of course, who will have to be kenneled, and my son, who will need to be either brought along or tended. And then of course there is the decision itself, a definitive commitment to some place exotic, which necessarily excludes all other exotic destinations, which brings me right back to square one.

This, says my friend, is the problem. With so much to choose from, she is afraid she will make the wrong choice. Selection is always exclusion, after all, and the censure of her friends who could not believe that she missed the Musee Rodin in Paris or the Tate Modern in London leaves her with a sense of compulsion mixed with guilt. Would it be so terrible if she didn't see the Turners at the National Gallery? The Venus de Milo at the Louvre? The leaning tower in Pisa? What if she just wanted to sit at a café in Tuscany and sip on an espresso?

What she'd like, my friend says, is to go back to the time when she was 19 and strolled through Europe with an Army-Navy backpack and a copy of "Let's Go! Europe" stuffed into her back Levi's pocket. She'd hop on a train and get off at the stop with the most euphonious name, stay in a hostel, grab a baguette and some Gruyere cheese and fall in with a couple who had a similar sense of adventure.

What happened to that sense of adventure, she wonders.

My friend stares at the crab grass poking out from her driveway and chides herself for letting the driveway project go so long. How can she dream of Florence when her driveway is parting like the Red Sea?

Last week I ran into a neighbor of mine whose wife has an incurable disease which flares and remits at uneven intervals. Christine's last bout with the illness was so dreadful that she told him all she wanted was her self back. When the illness finally loosed its grip, she told him to quit his job and spend a year on their boat. She did not know when the illness would strike again, she said, and she did not want to spend her ailing days remembering the front-loading washer they had just bought, what she wanted to remember was the time they spent together as a family.

What could Christine tell my friend about time and priorities, I wonder. What could she tell her about negotiating between the demands of roofs and driveways, washing machines and vinyl siding? No doubt she would have much to say about the toll that a drawer full of dreams takes on a mind that yearns to wander.

Unpublished

ESSAYS, SPEECHES

The Language of Time

I am thinking, as I often do these days, of a painting.

The painting is Claude Monet's "Gare Saint-Lazare: Arrival of a Train." Monet painted it in 1877, still very much under the spell of British painters John Constable and J.M.W. Turner, to whom he was artistically indebted. Few artists knew the fugitive nature of fog as well as Turner, and fewer, like Constable, appreciated the ephemeral nature of time as well as Constable.

The Gare Saint-Lazare is now the second busiest train station in Paris just after the cavernous Gare du Nord. Monet wasn't the only Impressionist drawn to it; Édouard Manet and Gustave Caillebotte both painted Impressionist scenes of the 1837 train station. Why wouldn't they? It was in their neighborhood, and with its great constellation of humanity, hubris and humidity gave the Impressionists everything they needed to incarnate their ideas about art.

I come back to Monet's painting because, in so many ways, it is a metaphor – in some respects *the* metaphor – of the modern age. Time, in its oppressive exactitude, is both meticulous and ambiguous. It was the railroads, as Tony Judt wrote recently in The New York Review of Books, which gave us the crushing precision of time. One no longer met at half-past the hour, but at 8:37 or 11:33. Railroads, as Monet implies, gave time an industrial brutality. And yet, and here is where the art meets philosophy, time itself is as evanescent and fleeting as ever. Never again will the sun strike the emerging steam with quite this hint of lavender. Only in this moment will the sky electrify with a lemon-lime haze. This thing that we attempt to hold and to hold ourselves to is fugacious and insubstantial.

We are, says Monet, in the Gare Saint Lazare, fooling ourselves to imagine otherwise.

That all of this can be imputed by a painting and that it happens to be a painting by one of the geniuses of art, and that that painter *happens* to be French, might merely be coincidental. Edward Hopper painted a gorgeous rail-road station at sunset, stunning for its use of horizontal bands of color and that quintessential Hopper anomie. But Monet's is different. Monet's is French. And that, I would submit, matters.

We talk a lot these days about the clash of civilization, about the clash of culture. This always makes me chuckle a bit, first because it implies that we know what culture is and second that we know something about the culture with which ours is apparently clashing.

And that brings me to my first point about how a lifetime of French courses changed my life: They made me see that there is such a concept as culture. They made me understand that it can be, in the most Cartesian sense, identified, catalogued and disseminated. They made me see that it is something to be esteemed, to be valued, to be considered as an integral part of a nation's identity. The study of French made me understand that culture was a force with which to be reckoned and to which to be indebted.

How?

I see advertisements these days for courses on the study of a language that one can learn in 6 weeks or six months.

Stick this CD into your car stereo or download this audio to your iPod and speak like Baudelaire by spring. I'm sure all these work very well and can only applaud those evangels of multilingualism for their heroic efforts. But it took me years and years to learn French, and still the full grasp of the language eludes me. It took years of stepping into the language, clothing myself with it and walking around in it to understand that a language is more than a language just as words are more than letters. A language carries with it a history and a character and an identity that imparts itself distinctly and indelibly on the speaker. A language may be our finest way of inculcating what I believe to be the most critical human quality on earth: Empathy.

Once I knew an old man who worked in the U.S. State Department for most of his life. At the end of his life he worked as a copy editor at a community newspaper with me, and frequently regaled me with outlandish tales of American diplomatic blunders. But one of his insights I have always carried with me. He said that Americans believe all people in other countries are Americans who speak a different language. Strip away the language and we're all the same.

Mistake.

Language is, as I like to say, the footprint of thought. But the fact that thought is bred of culture and language is only a small part of that culture. I can remember walking to school every day in Angers, France, past walls and churches and school yards and universities that had been there for hundreds of years. During my first weeks in Angers, as this history began to seep into me, I thought what a burden it must be to grow up in a place where so much has been done before, where giants of literature and philosophy and art have already made the discoveries you could never hope to discern. Was that what gave all the young Frenchmen I saw that sense of *je m'enfouism*, that distinctly Gallic shrug?

But the more I stayed in Angers, the more I felt a sense of what the French call *autrefois* grounding me, making me aware of where I was and what this place and its history had contributed to the world. I began to feel a sense of alignment with time that I think is missing in the United States.

Our world today – and this is what I think Monet anticipates so beautifully – is the triumph of speed over thought. It is a word where 'yesterday' is not a rhapsodic indulgence of nostalgia but an epithet for obsolescence. "Oh, that's so yesterday," we say, as if yesterday itself were an assault on the present. But yesterday has its place and the French, I think, understand that.

When I first went to France in 1983, I was shocked that my adoptive parents, then only in their late 50s, were already retired. What on earth would they do with their time, I thought. As an American, time is spent, not passed. And it is spent generally by toil intended to earn more income, to spend more time in a treadmill of Sisyphean absurdity.

But in France, as my French parents demonstrated, time passes with your involvement. It matters that from Monday to Thursday the growth of your lilacs, though nearly imperceptible, was growth. It matters that the plums this year were sweeter than last and therefore must be consumed with deliberation and commentary. It matters that the light passed gently over the table in late spring, sending sparks of light from the tea kettle dappling over the fibers of the lemony carpet. Outside, the chickadee pressed its beak into the stale crust of bread that Monsieur had fitted into the feeder. One wondered if it were the same chickadee as was there yesterday. One wondered where he would go next.

How would my French parents spend their final years? In time that mattered, in moments such as this.

Maybe what Monet captured in the Gare Saint Lazarre was that French sense of time, the appreciation of moments as they are seen fleetingly because moments evaporate so swiftly.

Did conjugating the verb avoir teach me this?

Probably not. But did reading Montaigne's essays, his discursive and fanciful attempt to discover who he was, affect my writing? Unequivocally. I know that, but do the thousands of bloggers out there, bleating away their most recent apercus, know that? Probably not. Probably not just as they likely do not understand how Descartes affected them, or Pascal, or, heaven help us, Louis Pasteur.

Well, you might say, this is all very good if what interests you are the steamy affairs of Abelard and Heloise, or the machinations of Catherine de Medici, or the implications of the Edict of Nantes. But what can it possibly tell you of the Afghans or the Coptics or the Han in China and Basques in Spain.

It may tell me nothing at all except that there is something to tell. Studying one language is hardly as noble as studying 12. But it opens a part of the brain sealed by monomania and xenophobia. Anytime we step into one culture, doors open to others, even if they are doors we do not walk through. Just knowing they are there can, or should, grace us with respect and curiosity.

And respect and curiosity are as fine an antidote to parochialism and chauvinism as any. In this clash of civilizations that we can hardly understand, they may be the only hope we have left.

Why read?

In 1947, George Orwell published a short essay called "Why I Write."

By that time, he had published *Animal Farm, Homage to Catalonia, Bookshop Memories, Burmese Days* and a gaggle of essays. Three years later he would, in response to growing Soviet totalitarianism, pen his great novel, *1984*.

It seemed a reasonable act, for this impassioned but level-headed man, to finally and cleanly address what he was about. And the essay is trademark Orwell, in his clear, direct, "windowpane" prose. He enumerates four specific reasons for writing, two of which ("sheer egoism" and "aesthetic enthusiasm") we are surprised to associate with Orwell, and two of which ("historical impulse" and "political purpose") we cannot separate out from him.

I thought about Orwell's seminal essay because in coming to your glorious library, the first thought that struck me is that it is a place where things are read. Often, it is a place where books are selected with the intention to be read. Regardless, I am fusty enough in my conventions and obstinate enough in my romanticism to still equate libraries with reading.

I know, of course, that all manner of events transpire here, from community meetings to Internet surfing, to DVD purloining and the like. But I persist in my sentimental belief that the pillars that uphold our libraries continue to be for the purpose of reading, which brings me to the point of my talk: Why do it?

In 2004, the National Endowment of the Arts published "Reading at Risk," which found that fewer than half of American adults read literature. The biggest drop in the activity occurred among those 18 to 24 years old.

"This report documents a national crisis," Dana Gioia decried. "Reading develops a capacity for focused attention and imaginative growth that enriches both private and public life. The decline in reading among every segment of the adult population reflects a general collapse in advanced literacy. To lose this human capacity - and all the diverse benefits it fosters - impoverishes both cultural and civic life."

You may be delighted to know then, that in a recent report, the NEA has reported that for the first time in more than 25 years, American adults are reading more literature and that the biggest increase among that group is in young adults, ages 18 to 24. So, civilization as we know it will not turn to dust.

Now you can thank Harry Potter or the Twilight series or the NEA's muscular "The Big Read" program, or perhaps the sheer kick in the pants that a report like "Reading at Risk" can engender. Shame is a great motivator.

But you are still left with the question: Why do it? That reading among Americans is critical to the social fiber of the nation is not mere cant, but is supported by research. Previous NEA research has shown that literary readers volunteer, attend arts and sports events, do outdoor activities, and exercise at higher rates than non-readers. Like newspaper readers, then, fiction readers are doers. They lubricate the gears of an otherwise sedentary and indolent society.

What's interesting about the NEA report, and was

much commented upon at the time of its release, is the emphasis on literature, and specifically fiction, as the measure by which we should judge our collective reading health.

I too would like to focus on fiction, if only because it is my preferred genre and also because the benefits of reading non-fiction seem obvious.

[I shouldn't be so cavalier about that. Not long after Guttenberg created the press that would revolutionize printing and democratize novels, those privileged few who had exclusive access to classical tests were not exactly thrilled. What would happen when 'the masses' got hold of the precious texts heretofore reserved for the elites? Well, reformation, revolution and widespread literacy, to name three.] No wonder they worried.

Thankfully, we got over that. Subsequently, culture has almost always allied reading with virtue. The virtuous man was the well-read man and the well-read man read only non-fiction for the simple reason that until the 18th century there was no such thing as a novel. There were classic tales of heroism and epic poetry but, until about 200 years ago, no novels. The novel emerges out of the Renaissance and Enlightenment, which, among many of its great gifts, gave us one with which we still wrestle: the preoccupation with self.

Fanny Burney, with her 1778 publication *Evelina*, is often credited with inventing the novel. Others credit Daniel Defoe. Others go further back and cite Madame de La Fayette's *Princesse de Clèves* of 1678 or Cervantes *Don Quixote*. Some go as far back as the 11th century *Tale of the Genji* (written, unsurprisingly, by a woman).

Academics may quibble, but for our purposes it is safe to say that the novel emerged as a new art form in England in the late 18th century and two things happened almost immediately: They were devoured and they were despised – even by those who penned them.

Novels were irresistible because they were fancy, and because they were fancy, they were ridiculed. A novel, after all, is a lie. It is a lie, I would argue, that tells a truth, but fundamentally, it is still a lie. And mendacity is about as far away from virtue as you can get. So roundly were novels disdained that their authors took pains to distance themselves from them.

One of the most successful novelists of the early 19th century, Maria Edgeworth, cited as inspiration even by the redoubtable Sir Walter Scott, insisted that her works were not novels but "Morality tales—the author not wishing to acknowledge a Novel." As she wrote her friend Fanny Robinson, "Though I am as fond of Novels as you can be I am afraid they act on the constitution of the mind as Drams do on that of the body."

Novels would make you go all funny in the head. One too many and you'll end up like Madame Bovary.

It would take Jane Austen, whose *Mansfield Park* was sneered at as a "mere novel," to set things straight.

Austen not only single-handedly ironed out the clumsiness of early novels, but she pokes fun as those who would mock them. It is the bunglers and the dupes, like the execrable Mr. Collins, who sneer at novels. The spunky and genuine Elizabeth Bennett makes no apologies for indulging them. Austen's irony gently but effectively slays the prejudice against the novel, but she does more. What Austen shows us is that novels offer their own education. And here we get to the question of why read at all.

Austen's novels seem to be romances – who marries who, who is spurned by whom. But they are essentially novels of education. They are, as Maria Edgeworth intended, morality tales, after a fashion. Heroes become less prideful; heroines become less prejudice. Both move to the middle. Austen famously said that she did not need great swaths of continents or grotesquely Gothic fantasies to create a novel. All she needed were four or five families in a country town.

Anne Tyler might say the same. So would John Cheever.

Why?

It's because in novels we are looking to see ourselves – but only just. We are looking to see someone not exactly like us, but near enough that we might indulge a fantasy of our own, settle a bet with ourselves about what our lives might be like if we were only a little more adventurous, a little less discrete, a smidgen more decorous, a good deal more wealthy.

"Tell the truth – but tell it slant," Emily Dickinson said. And in novels we see ourselves slant, we see bewitching possibilities and harrowing escapes. We see versions of ourselves, elements of ourselves. We see our neighbors and we see our cousins. We see that we are not, as it can feel in our most despairing moments, singular, but share in this one essential human quest: What we want is to be understood.

I was 22 when I read Carson McCullers' *The Heart is a Lonely Hunter*. She was 23 when she wrote it. I was alone in a decaying Northeastern industrial city, living in a rented room up a pine-covered hill from a dog track. I saw myself as Mick, the lonely hunter who implausibly finds herself bewitched by a beauty she cannot articulate. So that is why we read, I thought. Not to know. Not to gather facts to impress and empower. Not to fortify ourselves with incontrovertible truths. But to see ourselves refracted. To see that we are not alone. We are all, I suspect, like Mick, magnetized by a beauty we can neither grasp nor express. We look, in literature, for those who will express it for us.

How is it that we all feel so much and articulate so little? We wonder, surely, about the same things: the mercilessness of tragedy, the injustice of cruelty, the bounty that seems so unmerited and the want that goes unquenched. Surely, we have all chewed a little on love—where to find it, how to hold on to it, what to do when it folds, fades or fissures? But most of us lack the gifts of language and imagination authors bestow on us. And so we feed off their understanding, their wit, even their confusion.

All wisdom, the Greeks believed, begins with wonder. I often fear that in a society in which everything is "so yesterday," we have become so jaded that we have gypped ourselves out of wonder. Without wonder, we do not dare. Without daring, we do not imagine. Without imagination, we do not move. Without movement, we atrophy. We atrophy socially, but we also atrophy emotionally. Our souls are limitless. Why choke their expansion?

Wonder is what makes me pick up a book and worm myself into the mind of a character I do not know but long to. Wonder is what draws me to books about experiences I could never have and would defy having. Reading helps me collapse continents and erase divisions. It reminds me that truth can encompass fact, but goes so much farther beyond.

But, most of all, I think reading underlines the uncomfortable reality that mortality prevents me from experiencing all that I might. I am limited by time, by resources, by geography, by responsibility. Ultimately, my nearest chance to learn about The Other is by reading about him. And in reading about him, and those like him, I develop the most critical human quality we can possess: Empathy.

I would like to think that I have the imaginative capacity to stand in the shoes of all who stand to gain or lose in this world, but I simply do not. Yet, reading helps me get there. When Montaigne writes, "I am, I know not how, double, even to myself," I understand what he means. When he writes, "I have never seen a greater monster or miracle in the world than myself," I think, "That's me!" The point, of course, is that it is all of us, that we are all monsters and miracles, consistencies and contradictions. Reading reminds us of that and to be reminded of our foibles and see ourselves refracted means that we are not alone, it means that we are somewhere understood. And it means that somewhere, through this mysterious mélange of imagination and empathy, we will have the opportunity to understand others – even those we meet only on the page.

I realize that this solution is not flawless. It is not guaranteed. But it is a beginning. And we need to start somewhere.

Spiritual Calls – Dramatic
and not so much

A friend of mine thinks he has heard the call.

He tells me this in a breathless, dewy-eyed way and for a minute, I feel a little twinge of envy.

Wouldn't it be nice, I think, to receive some lightning strike revelation, some Paul on the road to Damascus Epiphany, where the road ahead of you is not only lucid and unmistakable, but divinely sanctioned? Wouldn't it be convenient – if John Calvin is correct about predestination – to have the veil on your destiny lifted and survey the yellow brick road before you with delicious certainty and the assurance that your path was divinely blessed? Think of all of the hapless bumbling that could be avoided, the absurdly maladroit stabs at personal direction we could circumvent? No more *Cosmo* quizzes on the beach. No more late-night conjecturing with equally clueless pals. No more frittering away our mortality on dead-ends.

My friend wants to do something marvelous and dramatic, as is the way of these grand revelations, and for a moment I fear he's gone a little batty. My friend wants to go to Central America. He wants to start a hospital for the poor. He wants to upend his life and reshape it, align it with the values that have lain too long dormant in his soul.

Why is it that spiritual calls always take you away

from your life rather than ground you in it?

Perhaps it is that destiny itself is a romantic ideal and the true romantic sees his future writ large in exotic lands, riding astride a camel or a yak, continents from sputtering along an Interstate in a Hyundai.

I have been thinking a lot lately about destiny and prophecy, perhaps because at 10, my son is at the age of the grand epic of Harry Potter, Narnia and the Phantom Tollbooth. The world seems an esoteric, mystifying place battered about by sharply divided notions of good and evil. The only way to navigate between these distinct banks is to discover the prophecy that is your road map.

"You have made us for yourself, O Lord. And our hearts and souls are restless until they rest in the."

That is St. Augustine, the 4th century bishop of Hippo who articulated that inquietude that underlies pretty well every book you'll find in the self-help section of the bookstore. We want to "Find Our Passion," "Discover Our Life's Purpose," "Live a Purpose-Driven Life," "Complete Our Legacy." We have an entire industry now of "Life Coaches" –therapists being woefully insufficient, to say nothing of old aunties—to act as divining rods of our souls.

There is something "out there" for us, something grand and noble and magnificent. We merely have to find the pathway, like Diogenes with his lamp, looking tenaciously for the truth.

I come from a faith tradition that doesn't brook much truck in destiny. The idea of destiny suggests there is a painless answer to the quibbles that befuddle us, and all we have to do is find the right key. The notion, as some would have it, that things are "meant to be," only works when things turn out well – or you have nothing better to say. Things are only "meant to be" in retrospect. We are

sense-seeking beings and so assign reasons to flukes that
have no bearing on reason at all. Things happens, and
then we find reasons for them having happened, thus
giving our life a narration that makes more sense going
backwards than it does going forward.

"We do not know how to pray as we ought," Paul tells
us, and by that I think he means that our whole definition
of prayer, to say nothing of its object, is very likely askew.
Most of the time, we don't pray; we petition. Scripture
encourage us to ask and so we ask away, pleading away
for relief of our anxieties or wisdom in our uncertain-
ties, a path forward when the future is obscure. I don't
besmirch these entreaties. What we want tells us much
about who we are.

How often do we pray to align our hearts with God's?
How often in prayer to we listen, and not just listen,
but hear. Why do we persist in thinking it must be a
thunderbolt, a Steven Spielberg epic, soundtrack by John
Williams? We think we know what God wants of us,
but I think most of our life is a search to unravel it. A
comprehended God, St John Chrysostom said, "is no
God." But most of us wish for a little more clarity, even
as we fear what that lucidity demands of us.

"I do not understand my own actions," muses Paul.
"I do not do what I want, but I do the very thing I hate."

And who hasn't felt that every once in a while?

******

They say that everyone has a talent. I am a great
admirer of talent, having so little of my own. I admire an
elegant table and a scarf worn with panache – gifts which
elude me. I admire good cooking and fine wood work, a
carpenter who can look at a warren and create a home.
And I admire a woman called Barbara, a woman whose
talent is quilting.

I cannot sew. I cannot take up a hem. I cannot knit, crochet or darn socks, so it is perhaps not unusual that I should admire Barbara, a woman who can make a quilt look like a field of wildflowers on July day.

I want to tell you about Barbara because earlier this year she did something marvelous, something my Jewish friends would call a mitzvah. And it started with death.

In addition to her quilting prowess, Barbara has a generous soul. It was that, I think, that led her to volunteer once a week in what we once used to quaintly refer to as an "old age home." Death is a constant guest in such a place, alternately shunned, feared, and sometimes, even welcomed. The folks who ran this particular home did what many do when death strikes. They covered it up. They ushered it out. If life came in the front door, the folks at this old-age home sent it out the back, like the garbage or like something of which we should be ashamed. When they came to their senses, and recognized their folly, they asked Barbara for their help.

The body of the dead needed to be embraced. The life of the deceased should be celebrated. The grieving needed to see death, not by omission but in glory. They asked Barbara to create a quilt for the dead and when she thought and prayed on it, she did. The quilt is a glorious pattern of the earth's seasons, with the wonderful quote from Ephesians to remind us all that there is a time for everything in life, even death, even mourning.

Barbara doesn't know the people who will be draped in the quilt over which she labored. But she knows now that people in that home will leave life the way they came into it – swaddled in color, and in love.

******

"Christianity, if false, is of no importance, and if true, of infinite importance. The only thing it cannot be is moderately important."

That is our friend C.S. Lewis, who would understand someone like Barbara. He would understand that Christianity does not always explode in bonfires of heroism but in sparks of quiet faith.

Those of us who are people of faith are forever "groaning," as St. Paul says, toward the life God wants for us. We seek so hard and so avidly that I think we miss the engines of mercy and the opportunities for compassion that slip by us every day.

We fool ourselves to think we have to leave our life to save it. We merely have to return to ourselves to see it.

It is that perpetual, incremental drip away from selfishness and toward selflessness that is our real epiphany. The drive to grandiosity, in faith or in career or in wealth, is, I think, a fatal kind of pride masking itself as humility.

I am a believer that faith, like love, takes practice. Just as we dream that love will be passionate and soul-enriching and blinding in its fervor, we wonder at what can seem the fecklessness of our faith. Where is the rhapsody? Where are the fireworks? Where is the thunderclap of recognition that will ignite the dramatic alteration in my life that will make me God's alone?

I would suggest that it was a *road* that leads to Damascus and that road is often pitted and pitched. It is filled with detours and divots and mud that seems immobilizing. Doubt sidelines us and leaves us weary. But look around. The days of others are brightened by your smile, their loads lessened by your hand. Every day comes with the opportunity to shed the weight that burdens us. Every day, we cast off temper and fear. Every day we see not only our own path, but the twisted, tortuous ones of others. Every morning, we have a chance to swaddle the dead and embrace the living. It is not grand. It is not pyrotechnic.

But the quiet poignancy of our quest is as elegant a testament to our faith as any thunderclap. Most of us dream of having our calling clear and dramatic, like St. Paul's. But the truth is subtler. Mot of us will hear the voice of God as Elijah did, not in the wind but in a whisper.

Thoughts on Art

Almost two years ago, a searing, knife-like pain in my abdomen sent me hurtling to the nearest hospital. By the time my husband completed that 7-mile journey, the pain was so intense that I was unable to speak beyond a single word: "Help." Although I did not know it, I was in the throes of the agony that comes from an unusual, and life-threatening medical emergency. My intestines had twisted on themselves, like ribbons coiling around a maypole. My innards were being strangled.

Fortunately for me, I had arrived in sufficient time for doctors to slice me open and correct the problem. A volvulus, I was told later, is a rather simple surgical fix: cut it out and stitch it up. But in the weeks and days that followed, as I vacillated between feelings of relief that the crisis had been averted and terror over how near to catastrophe I had come, a single image kept materializing in my mind.

The image was Giotto's "The Visitation," an early 14th century depiction of the moment when, as related by Luke, the Virgin Mary, pregnant with Jesus, goes to visit her cousin Elizabeth, who is herself pregnant with John the Baptist. Why this image – or any artistic work – would cleave to me post-surgically was a mystery I could not unravel, any more than I could stop the Giotto from coming to mind. It was as ineradicable as it was enigmatic.

It was not the first time that an image would stay with

me, like the scent of a perfume, but I had understood the reasons other works had stayed with me. This persistence left me baffled.

It wasn't until I zeroed in on the aspect of the work that fixated me most that I began to understand the persistence of the image. What got me was the gaze. What got me was how the women locked into one another. It is the locked, intimate gaze of two women linked by spirit, by destiny, by understanding. Mary looked at Elizabeth and in an instant, Elizabeth got it.

She got it. In the story, Mary not only knows who she is carrying, but knows he will meet a violent end, just as Elizabeth knows her son will meet a similar fate. The two women are the only ones on earth who can understand the joy and the anguish that will be theirs. They *get* each other.

And that is what we look for in life – not to be separate from one another, but to be understood, emotionally embraced on a level that transcends thought. Giotto captured that spiritual simpatico, and when I understood that, I understood what I needed.

I wanted someone to understand. I wanted someone to get it.

I wonder if we have all had moments like that. Not moments where we feel misunderstood and hunger for empathy, which is, in many respect, part of the human condition, but moments where we what we feel cannot be encapsulated by the hard precision of words, but is best articulated by something beyond words, something that we see. Art fills in those interstices.

How many of us, for instance, have felt that the world is not the linear, reliable compass that we pretend it to be, but an arresting and sometimes frightening collision of reality and imagination, the logical and the absurd? How many of us have seen the long, lozenge-like plains of Mark Rothko and sensed, that we have been there, in the honeyed sunset of a drawing day, or the bleak, inky black tar of a despairing mood we cannot shake?

You can say all you will about art elevating our senses and exhilarating our public discourse, about it enlivening our public spaces and feeding our spirit. But I think the best art begins at the place where words leave off. The best art enunciates the ineffable qualities about living and about what it is to be a soul in an all-too material world.

I like to tell people that when I began reporting on art a dozen years ago about all I knew was that Renoir painted dogs and Mary Cassatt made the best Mother's Day cards. That wasn't expressly true, exactly. I had the better-than-average understanding of art that comes standard in French majors. I could tell a Degas from a De Kooning and a Gainsborough from a van Gogh, but much of what I needed to learn would come from seeing. Much of what I needed to say about art was leaving myself open to the distinct possibility that I knew nothing at all.

Fortunately, finding oneself underprepared for one's task is not unusual in journalism. Reporters are forever being thrust into some arcane maelstrom or other they must assess, decipher, critique and resolve in al the time it takes to make a king size bed. But I didn't want to do that with art because in spite of my professed ignorance, I didn't think art deserved it. Art deserved better than my understanding of it and that required two indispensible attributes from me. One was curiosity. And the other was humility.

I don't pretend to be Michael Kimmelman of the *New York Times* or Blake Gopnik of *Newsweek*. These are art critics of unique focus and uncommon eloquence. I am a reporter for a medium-sized weekly newspaper, sharing with my readers some of the jolts and insights I receive from a artwork too breezily dismissed from media outlets content to assuage their journalistic guilt with a four-column photograph and a two sentence caption. The visual arts, like music or dance, have largely been excised from newspapers like mine. Their owners are certain in their presumptions that what readers want is more television news, more celebrity squibs, more nonsense about purveyors of nonsense. And it is through this calculus that we all become smaller.

I do not pretend expertise in my area. But I do keep with me the virtues of humility and curiosity.

Humility in face of a Caravaggio is easy to come by, particularly from someone as aesthetically inept as I. How can you not stare and gape at the pained, disillusioned look of abandonment that crosses Jesus' face in despair over his betrayal by Judas? Religion aside, who has not been betrayed by a friend? Who has not felt that poisonous mix of disbelief and rage?

Oh, but many cannot. Many are unable. Many, too many, are unmoved. I often wonder whether we do not always know what we are feeling or why because we have never really put ourselves in front of a piece of art that might elicit the very emotion that we are at pains to name.

When I began to tackle the art beat, I drew strength from something I learned a long time ago by a teenage piano prodigy whom I interviewed for a weekly community newspaper. My subject was soon to be off to Juilliard and a bright and auspicious future. I asked her a rather standard question I asked of these young wunderkinds, which was whether she believed her proficiency at piano was a gift. She shook her head. No, she said. It's not the playing that is a gift. It is the ability to appreciate the music that is the real gift.

The comment struck me as insightful from such a

young subject – underlining the inevitability that her future was going to be more brilliant than any I could hope for. Unless you loved Bach, it was impossible to say it was a gift to play him well. If you couldn't swoon over Mozart, all the digital dexterity in the world would never compensate. It was the ability to fall in love with beauty that was the most precious gift. It was the ability to marvel.

Appreciation is one of those banal, platitudinous words that gets invoked in greeting cards, gut academic courses and clumsy expressions of gratitude, but has been defused of all its vitality. It seems facile and obvious. But being able to appreciate beauty – in this case, art – is not as reflexive as we'd like to imagine. It requires a quality that many of us in this post-modern, archly ironic age seem to lack. It requires awe.

The Greeks believed that wonder is the first step toward wisdom. But many of us in this been-there-done-that age of tweets, jabs, slow-mo, fast-forward, delete age have lost that ability. We have lost the capacity to wonder. And without it, we cannot see. Without it, we are blind, feeling in the dark for some kind of transcendence that continues to elude us.

Years ago, I was lucky enough to attend a recital by the soprano Kiri Te Kanawa at the Kennedy Center in Washington, D.C. Seats were hard to come by and so I was awarded only one ticket by the press office and I went alone, in my single seat, then knowing very little of Te Kanawa and less of Strauss. And all alone, in my single seat, I heard music come out of Te Kanawa that I never before imagined could have emerged from a human mouth. I realized, in my aural enchantment, that I had thought a good deal of what God looked like before, or what he felt like, but never until that night had I imagined what he might *sound* like. When I listened to Te Kanawa, I knew.

Art had filled my sensory gap.

We are fed by food and liquid nourishes our thirst, but what quells our yearning for beauty? What, for that matter, sates our appetite for ugliness, for, surely, as a violent world attests, we have that craving too? But I don't believe we give that artistic hunger sufficient attention. It is, I suspect, like a spiritual hunger that we sate with empty promises and ephemeral illusions. After awhile, like most hunger, it becomes so much a part of us that we hardly notice.

Two thousand years ago, Pontius Pilate snidely asked a young upstart, "What is truth," and from at least that point on we've continued to wrestle with the question. Perhaps one of the most endearing qualities of art to me, as an interested observer, is that Pilate's question is the very riddle with which it tussles, too. Art, of course, is not truth, as Picasso reminded us, but it is "the lie that makes us realize truth."

And like truth, art comes hurtling toward us, destabilizing us in ways that confound our certainties and threaten our convictions. It assaults us, addles us and astonishes us. I remember standing in front of George Stubbs massive Horse Attacked by a Lion in Library Court of the British Art Center. It's a big and pretty grisly scene: a lion leaps out of the wilderness and gouges its teeth into the glorious, butterscotch hide of a fleeing horse. I could not move away from this painting and I could not discern what it was about it that was keeping me transfixed.

It came to me in my sympathy for the wounded horse that this dynamic battle between wildness and domestication, ferocity and docility, was, in a sense, my battle, the battle between discipline and rapacity, the visceral and cerebral, the savage and the tame. It is, in a sense, the battle of all of us in a civilized world and Stubbs captured it in this bloodthirsty homage to two beasts in a struggle that would leave one of them dead and one of them sated.

My money was on the lion.

So here was an expression of truth from an unlikely source. But I have found it, too, in the abstract emotiveness of Hugh O'Donnell, in the fiery poetry of Miro, in the shattering juxtapositions of Dali and in the super-human grace of Fra Angelico. I had never though too very much about the way we try to contain and organize the flotsam of our lives until I looked at a Joseph Cornell box. I had never considered what it was to see a whole way of life dematerializing before your eyes until I found Turner. I had never known, really known, what it was to grieve until I saw Rembrandt's last self-portrait.

"The stupid believe that to be truthful is easy," Willa Cather wrote. "Only the artist, the great artist, knows how difficult it is."

I often have to remind myself that what I am looking at is marble, or paint or clay. I have to shake myself to recall that what I am looking at is deception that looks very much like truth. But deception in service to truth is only a parable by another name. As Magritte said, "Art evokes the mystery without which the world would not exist."

And if that shakes up our world, so much the better. Imagine the wonder of having beauty, real beauty, and land smack in front of you. You could hardly blame yourself for chasing after it the rest of your life.